"At last! A work on the fruit of the Spirit that takes you past mere definitions to simple yet profound application. In *Flourish*, Ava Pennington walks us through the garden of faith to examine the fruit of the Spirit. Like a master gardener, she combines the tools of Scripture, story, and application to help us cultivate the fruit by which we become more like Christ. With each chapter she helps you to recapture your sense of awe and wonder at the fruit God deeply desires us to have and to share with others. After twenty-plus years of pastoral ministry experience, I am excited to recommend *Flourish* for anyone wishing to grow and mature in the fruit of the Spirit. Pick up the book and invite in the Holy Spirit."

—Michael Thedford, pastor of LifeQuest Church,
Palm City, Florida

"After years of serving as a pastor, I came to the uncomfortable realization that while I saw the gifts of the Spirit emphasized, the fruit of the Spirit was woefully neglected. As both a spiritual shepherd and an individual Christ follower, I began pursuing a greater understanding and application of that fruit and searched for resources to help me nurture its growth in both my life and my congregation's. Ava Pennington's *Flourish* is exactly that kind of resource. In her easy-to-read style, Ava brings understanding and practical application to her readers as they partner with the Holy Spirit to see abundant fruitfulness in their lives. I look forward to sharing this wonderful book with many fellow Christians in years to come."

—Jim Reed, lead pastor of New Life Community Church,
Danville, Virginia

"I remember a time when just thinking about the fruit of the Spirit overwhelmed me. Ava Pennington's grace-centered practices lower the branches of love, joy, peace, patience, kindness, goodness, faithfulness, gentleness, and self-control. She brings the fruit within reach for those seeking to grow a deeper relationship with Christ. Having this resource years ago would have fast-tracked my intimacy with the

Lord. I highly recommend *Flourish* and greatly appreciate Ava's heart to help believers live abundantly in Christ."

—Linda Goldfarb, speaker, author, and certified life coach

"Ava Pennington's work never fails to draw me in with its story, humor, and depth. She easily takes us to the deepest places where God waits for us to know Him, know more about Him, and love Him in ways we've yet to discover. Sitting with Ava's work is one of life's pleasures."

—Eva Marie Everson, CEO of Word Weavers International and award-winning author and speaker

"In *Flourish*, author Ava Pennington gives us an incredible gift—a road map to an abundant life. Set in a strong foundation of biblical truth, her practical tips and relatable stories provide both hope and solid help as we navigate through life. I already know this book will become dog-eared with loving use. And it's a treasure I'll share with others to help them along the way."

—Edie Melson, award-winning author and director of the Blue Ridge Mountains Christian Writers Conference

"I have read many books on the fruit of the Spirit and can easily name the nine attributes we receive from the Holy Spirit to become more like Christ. Ava Pennington, however, goes deeper and shows how the enemy attempts to stunt our spiritual growth to keep us from experiencing the full blessing of our Christlike characteristics. The author doesn't leave us hanging with hopelessness; rather, she gives us the spiritual weapons we need to stand strong and firm against the thief who comes to steal and destroy."

—Crystal Bowman, author of more than one hundred books, including *Our Daily Bread for Kids*

# Flourish

# Flourish

## GRACE-CENTERED PRACTICES TO PROTECT AND GROW A FRUITFUL LIFE IN CHRIST

Ava Pennington

*Flourish: Grace-Centered Practices to Protect and Grow a Fruitful Life in Christ*


Published by Kregel Publications, a division of Kregel Inc., 2450 Oak Industrial Dr. NE, Grand Rapids, MI 49505. www.kregel.com.



Ava Pennington is represented by and *Flourish* is published in association with The Steve Laube Agency, LLC. www.stevelaube.com.



Cataloging-in-Publication Data is available from the Library of Congress.

ISBN 978-0-8254-5561-2, print
ISBN 978-0-8254-5563-6, epub
ISBN 978-0-8254-5562-9, Kindle

Printed in the United States of America
25 26 27 28 29 30 31 32 33 34 / 5 4 3 2 1

*To the memory of my husband, Russ—*
*you were the Lord's gift to me,*
*daily demonstrating the fruit of the Spirit*
*both intentionally and unintentionally.*
*I was, am, and will be forever blessed by your love.*

# Contents

CHAPTER 1

# The Status Quo Has Got to Go!

The squirrels beat me to the fruit . . . again.

Living in Florida, I've learned that the sweetest fruit grows right in my own backyard: oranges, pineapples, even mangoes. Especially mangoes. My mouth waters every spring as I watch blossoms develop into fruit on our two mango trees. Tiny orbs smaller than golf balls slowly mature into the sweetest mangoes I've ever tasted—that is, when I actually get to them.

Unfortunately, the squirrels often reach them first. Fruit from trees I cultivated, watered, and fertilized. Fruit I diligently watched as it ripened from green to an inviting shade of yellow-orange. Fruit from which I've inhaled a sweet fragrance proclaiming readiness to be harvested and enjoyed.

One of the great frustrations in growing fruit is watching it develop day by day, only to see it stolen just as it reaches the peak of ripeness. I'd look up to see half-eaten fruit still hanging high on the tree out of my reach, yet not out of the reach of agile squirrels hopping from branch to branch—brazen thieves taunting me as they snatch their mouthwatering treasures.

Even if mangoes are not your thing, you may still recall biting into a ripe piece of fruit on a hot summer day. Maybe it was a peach, a plum, or a slice of watermelon. Remember the sweet taste as the juice dripped off your chin?

These are not the only types of fruit we're meant to enjoy. God describes several of His attributes as fruit He develops in us. The apostle Paul listed these in Galatians 5:22–23: love, joy, peace, patience, kindness, goodness, faithfulness, gentleness, and self-control. They are not separate fruits (plural). Rather, each one is a display or facet of the fruit (singular) the Holy Spirit grows in our lives. We don't have the option of choosing which ones we like or want. They come as a package of nine. God develops this fruit in us to grow us to be more like Christ. So why do we often feel as if we don't have enough of this fruit? Perhaps it's because this fruit is also the target of a thief.

## Spiritual Thievery

The fruit of the Spirit is ours at the moment of faith when the Holy Spirit takes residence in those who receive Jesus as Lord and Savior.[1] Through His presence, He continuously works in each of us to graciously provide both His forgiveness and the characteristics of Christlikeness.

Still, many of us lack these qualities—qualities we were meant to have in abundance. How often have you and I wished we had greater peace or more patience? Or mourned our lack of self-control? How many times have we longed to be more loving or agonized over the joy stealers in life? What happened to the abundant life Jesus declared for us? Many believers know what God has promised, yet are frustrated because of their lack of progress.

The Bible describes Satan as an accuser, tempter, roaring lion, and serpent.[2] In John 10:10, Jesus spoke of the thief who comes to steal, kill, and destroy—speaking a rebuke against the religious leaders who failed to recognize Jesus as the source of abundant life. Jesus was also clear about whom those leaders belonged to: "You are of your father the devil . . . a murderer . . . and the father of lies" (John 8:44). Their thievery came naturally from Satan, their spiritual father.

When Satan is at work, the result can be a discouraging sense of half-eaten fruit hanging on the branches of our lives. The fruit is there, but we're cheated out of the full blessing of watching these characteristics fully ripen in us as we live out our Christian faith.

Still, we're not left helpless as the thief schemes to spoil our precious birthright. Just as the Bible speaks of fruit and thieves, it also reveals that God has always been in the recovery business.

- In Genesis 14:14–16, Abraham led the defeat of the four kings to rescue Lot.
- In Exodus 13, the Lord equipped Moses to lead the Israelites out of Egyptian slavery.
- In Romans 8:1–2, we read about the greatest recovery mission of all time, when Jesus set us free from the law of sin and death.

## The Power to Steal or Stunt?

A twenty-year corporate career in the financial district of New York City trained me to be goal oriented. And the way to achieve my goals was to try harder, work smarter, and do better. I needed to learn that growing and maturing the fruit of the Spirit is not simply a function of doubling down on my efforts. Instead, the answer was to change my perspective. As theologian and author J. I. Packer noted, "The Christian's life . . . is supernatural; only the Spirit can initiate and sustain it."[3]

Trying harder while depending on our own efforts is not effective. What *is* effective is surrendering to the Holy Spirit. But this does not mean we sit back and abdicate our responsibility. The apostle James wrote, "Submit therefore to God. But resist the devil, and he will flee from you" (James 4:7). It's not one or the other, it's both: submission *and* resistance.

As authors Neil T. Anderson and Robert L. Saucy note, "Faith calls for our participation. . . . Living by faith means acting in faith. Some people say that our response should be passive since the Christian life is in reality Christ living His life in us through the empowerment of the Spirit. That we should just wait for God's power to act. But faith is an active concept, and living by faith requires us to live in obedience to God."[4] We can say, "I'm yours, Lord. Have your way in my life." But we harvest the fruit of the Spirit when our actions match our words.

Author Jerry Bridges describes it this way: "I misconstrued dependence on the Holy Spirit to mean I was to make no effort, that I had no responsibility. I mistakenly thought if I turned it all over to the Lord, He would make my choices for me. . . . But this is not God's way. He makes provision for our holiness, but He gives us the responsibility of using those provisions."[5]

We don't have the power to create the fruit of the Spirit, regardless of how much effort we expend. Only the Holy Spirit, the third person of the Trinity, can do that. And since God alone can create this fruit, Satan does not have the authority or the ability to steal what the Holy Spirit has planted in us. However, our spiritual enemy doesn't need to actually *steal* the mature fruit. All that's required is to stunt its growth, preventing it from maturing. Similar to a natural fruit tree, immature fruit drops off the branches of our lives, littering the ground with unripe fruit that will never reach its potential. But we play a part in this process. Author, speaker, and photographer Edie Melson explains, "Without transformation, information is just extra baggage. It is our responsibility to apply the things God speaks into our lives."[6] Trying harder in our own strength focuses on external behavior modification. But spiritual transformation focuses on surrender to the Holy Spirit. However, don't mistake surrender for passivity. Surrender is intentional and active!

Have you ever eaten unripe fruit? Unlike juicy, tasty, and satisfying ripe fruit, immature fruit is usually dry, bitter, and unsatisfying. Call our spiritual fruit stolen or stunted, diminished, damaged, or spoiled, the result is the same. We're cheated out of fully experiencing all the Holy Spirit prepared for us to enjoy. So what can we do to protect the crop of our fruit from enemy attack? How can we nurture good fruit in an evil world ruled by the devil?

## How Powerful Is Satan?

When we think of our spiritual enemy, we can be ensnared by either of two opposite—yet equally harmful—mistakes. The first is to think Satan is equal to or greater in power than God. The other is to think the devil is merely a fable: a caricature with horns and a tail, dressed in a red jumpsuit and toting a pitchfork.

Biblical reality corrects these misconceptions while providing both comfort and a challenge. Satan is a created being—a fallen angel. While God is omnipotent (all-powerful), omniscient (all-knowing), and omnipresent (present everywhere at the same time), Satan has none of these attributes. But he is still a formidable and unrelenting foe. The name *Satan* derives from a Hebrew word commonly translated as "adversary." He's an adversary we should neither overestimate nor underestimate. But we have the assurance that "greater is He who is in [us] than he who is in the world" (1 John 4:4).

God has granted Satan limited, temporary authority in our world. And once, outside of Christ, we were like prisoners of war (POWs) under that authority. The apostle Paul used similar POW imagery in Colossians 1:13 to describe our release: God "rescued us from the domain of darkness, and transferred us to the kingdom of His beloved Son." Jesus was also clear that the devil is already cast out and judged.[7] We are free! So if we're free, why do we still struggle? Both the apostle Peter and James told us to resist the devil.[8] And God's Word would not tell us to do something if it were impossible to do it.

Then what prevents us from resisting the devil—from standing against the devil's attacks on the fruit God promises us by His Spirit?

## The Power of Abiding

While we cannot create fruit, we can position ourselves for the Holy Spirit to have His way with us. Only one position can accomplish this: the place of abiding. In John 15:4–5, Jesus told His disciples, "Remain in Me, and I in you. Just as the branch cannot bear fruit of itself but must remain in the vine, so neither can you unless you remain in Me. I am the vine, you are the branches; the one who remains in Me, and I in him bears much fruit, for apart from Me you can do nothing."

What does abiding in Christ look like in daily life? To abide is to live in, to dwell. To remain connected—permanently. A branch does not alternately attach to and detach from the trunk, back and forth depending on the occasion. It must remain connected for life to flow uninterrupted. Abiding requires total and consistent dependence on the Lord. This process of abiding reflects an ongoing prayer life and an intentional decision to be aware of His presence in and with us throughout our day. Brother Lawrence, a seventeenth-century French monk, called this "the practice of the presence of God"—a lifestyle, whether deep in prayer or in the kitchen cooking dinner.

Satan does not have the authority to steal what the Holy Spirit has already provided. Still, our spiritual enemy can tempt us to neglect our abiding. Just as a branch broken from the vine no longer receives sustenance to bear fruit, our failure to remain connected separates us from everything we need to mature the Spirit's fruit in us. And our spiritual enemy employs a variety of weapons to accomplish this goal.

## The Enemy's Arsenal

The apostle Paul understood our need to be alert and aware of Satan's scheming character.[9] The enemy's arsenal includes two common tactics.

### *1. Tempting Us to Doubt God's Word*

Satan wants us to doubt God. Just as in the garden with Eve, he starts with a subtle question: "Has God really said . . . ?" (Genesis 3:1).

Pride can cause us to think we are more alert than Eve to the enemy's schemes. But consider what happens when we fail to experience the full fruit of the Spirit. What happens when we *don't* experience joy, peace, patience, self-control, and the rest? We hear Satan's whispered lies: *Could it be God can't be trusted? What if He didn't mean what He said?*

When I read God's Word and fail to recognize the reality of His promises in my life, it's way too easy for me to begin to doubt God. Way too easy for me to elevate the reality of my experience over the reality of God's reliability. After all, if one promise in the Bible doesn't seem dependable, how can I trust everything else God has said?

### *2. Attacking When We're Most Vulnerable*

I love watching nature documentaries—until they broadcast scenes of predators sneaking up on their prey. A lion watches a herd of gazelles from a distance and identifies a weak member, perhaps young or sick. In a flash, the predator charges. Even as the herd flees, the target is isolated and killed in a heartbreaking attack.

It's no coincidence the apostle Peter used the imagery of a prowling lion to describe Satan. We become vulnerable to the enemy's attacks when we pridefully overestimate our ability to withstand temptation. For example, people recovering from alcoholism may visit a bar with friends, confident in their ability to limit themselves to nonalcoholic beverages, only to fail.

Pride isn't the only emotion that leaves us open to attack. Shame is equally effective. If the tactic of doubting God's ability to keep His promises doesn't work, the enemy will shift our focus from the Father to ourselves. Failure often leads to discouragement and shame. I can try hard to "get it right" in my own strength and miss the mark. When that happens, my focus may become all about *me* to an unhealthy extreme. *I'm a failure. I'm worthless. What's the point of trying if I'm never going to get it right?* That unbalanced focus on ourselves leaves God out of the equation. We've ignored His power. His forgiveness. His equipping. And we become spiritual prey.

You would think we'd be alert to the enemy's strategies by now. We should be, right? But Satan fights dirty. A student of human nature from the beginning of creation, he targets our blind spots, our weaknesses, and our deepest self-focused desires. And we fall for his tricks again and again.

The enemy wants us to forget he is already defeated. God's Word reminds us the reason the Son of God appeared was to destroy the devil's work.[10] The war was won at the cross. Still, the devil continues to fight skirmishes until Christ returns for His own. Until that day, our spiritual enemy will do everything possible to cause us to live in defeat. The worst of it is, we help him do it.

## Does the Devil Make Us Do It?

Years ago, classic comedian Flip Wilson became famous for his tagline, "The devil made me do it!" He rose to fame as that line drew laughs from all who viewed his act. Unfortunately, what started as a joke has become an excuse to shift the blame from ourselves and our own choices.

The devil cannot *make* us do anything. However, if we let down our guard, the father of lies can use deceit to tempt us with our natural desires. Satan constantly works to draw us away from submission to the Holy Spirit, thus stunting the growth of the Spirit's fruit. We can blame the devil for sin in the world, but it's critical that we acknowledge our part in following his enticements. The apostle John divided our vulnerability into three areas: "the lust of the flesh and the lust of the eyes and the boastful pride of life."[11] The better we understand how we are lured away in these areas, the more alert and equipped we will be to withstand their temptations and cultivate the fruit the Holy Spirit intends us to have. But we need the right weapons.

## Spiritual Battles Require Spiritual Weapons

In Westerns and crime dramas, occasionally a character brings a knife to a gunfight. We understand the implication. In real life, at least, the person with the knife will lose to the one carrying a gun.

In spiritual battles, Christians frequently "bring a knife to a gunfight." God has given us so much better—everything we need to stand in victory. But how often do we ignore His provision and instead rush blindly into spiritual battle? We fail to properly arm ourselves, then wonder why we're defeated.

The apostle Paul, writing to the early church in Ephesus, described the "full armor of God" available for us to "stand firm against the schemes of the devil" (Ephesians 6:11). The word *schemes* is a translation of the Greek *methodeía*. It sounds like our English word *method*, doesn't it? However, *schemes* is much more sinister, alluding to cunning deception. It's an apt description of our enemy's methods!

God's armor equips us to overcome those methods. Paul listed the armor's components in Ephesians 6:13–17:

> Take up the full armor of God, so that you will be able to resist on the evil day, and having done everything, to stand firm. Stand firm therefore, having belted your waist with truth, and

> having put on the breastplate of righteousness, and having strapped on your feet the preparation of the gospel of peace; in addition to all, taking up the shield of faith with which you will be able to extinguish all the flaming arrows of the evil one. And take the helmet of salvation and the sword of the Spirit, which is the word of God.

Each element of God's armor serves a purpose. Truth and righteousness are woven into who we are and how we live. Faith, the assurance of salvation, and a solid foundation based on the Word of God are critical for us to be on guard against the enemy's schemes. All of these, working together, equip us to resist the devil and his work in our lives.

It's no coincidence that before listing the components of the armor, Paul exhorted his readers to be filled with the Holy Spirit. He painted a word picture to illustrate the life we settle for compared to the life our heavenly Father offers us in Jesus Christ. We can be controlled by wine, resulting in excessive sensual indulgence, or we can be filled—controlled—by God's precious and powerful Holy Spirit.[12] The choice is ours.

Intentional, willing, and joyful submission to the Holy Spirit is the key. Again and again the Bible reminds us that everything we accomplish of eternal value is through the Holy Spirit. Be encouraged by these verses:

> To Him who is able to do far more abundantly beyond all that we ask or think, according to the power that works within us, to Him be the glory. (Ephesians 3:20–21)

> It is God who is at work in you, both to desire and to work for His good pleasure. (Philippians 2:13)

> His divine power has granted to us everything pertaining to life and godliness, through the true knowledge of Him who called us by His own glory and excellence. (2 Peter 1:3)

## Why the Need for Spiritual Battle?

How does all this specifically relate to the fruit of the Spirit?

When the Bible was written, there were no chapter breaks or verse numbers. Paul's letter to the church in Ephesus was just that: a letter. Earlier in it, he wrote about the grace of salvation, the unity of the church body, and the importance of orderly relationships. He specifically referred to the priorities of preserving our relationships with each other in the unity of the Holy Spirit as well as being filled with the Spirit.[13] With this foundation, Paul then moved into instructions on how to successfully withstand the devil's schemes. Since it's the Spirit who produces fruit in us, the devil logically targets spiritual fruit with spiritual warfare.

For much of my life, I tried to cultivate the fruit of the Spirit because I wanted to be a better person. I wanted others to see me as more loving, patient, and kind. I wanted to be known as a good and faithful person, because, well, that's what Christians are supposed to be. I wanted to be the best Christian I could be.

Did you notice how many times the pronoun *I* appears in the previous paragraph? Six times in four sentences. *I* had missed the point. The fruit of the Spirit isn't intended for me to feel better about myself. Each of the nine displays of fruit serves two primary purposes. First, for us to become more like Christ to give Him the glory among His people. Second, to grow us as vessels through which the Lord blesses others. After all, a tree does not feed on its own fruit. Rather, it produces fruit to feed others.

It's time to take back and own what the Lord has promised us, giving God the glory.

## A Fourfold Approach

Join me as we examine each facet of the fruit of the Spirit through a fourfold approach.

### *1. Recognize the Enemy's Tactics*

Successful warfare requires an awareness of our own vulnerabilities. It also requires an understanding of the opponent's tactics. Satan is sneaky, and lies are some of his most potent weapons. But Jesus called Himself "the truth."[14] God has revealed everything we need to see through the lies and stop the plunder of our fruit. When we identify the enemy's modus operandi, we can repair what is broken and shore up our defenses with the help of the Holy Spirit.

Of course, as we've already observed, the devil can't force us to do anything we don't want to do. So why is he so successful at tempting us in ways that attack the fruit of the Spirit? Perhaps it's because he appeals to our old nature. The nature in which pride and selfishness rule. Sadly, the enemy doesn't have to work very hard to stunt the growth of our fruit. All too often we do it to ourselves.

### *2. Nurture a Right Perspective*

The thief operates successfully because he frequently has a better understanding than we do of how God grows His fruit in our lives. God's perspective is often different from ours. As the prophet Isaiah wrote in Isaiah 55:8–9:

> "For My thoughts are not your thoughts,
> Nor are your ways My ways," declares the LORD.
> "For as the heavens are higher than the earth,
> So are My ways higher than your ways
> And My thoughts than your thoughts."

Remember our earlier discussion of the armor of God? Did you notice that all the components of the armor are defensive except one? The only offensive item in Paul's list is the sword of the Spirit—the Word of God.[15] If we want to nurture a right perspective, it's critical to understand God's perspective, found in His Word. We'll explore each aspect of the fruit of the Spirit and how He cultivates His fruit in us.

### *3. Recover and Grow*

A recovery mission is the next step after we experience defeat. As we apply biblical principles in surrender to the Holy Spirit, we'll be better equipped to guard our hearts, recover what the thief has attacked, and nurture new growth.

First Corinthians 10:13 reminds us:

> No temptation has overtaken you except something common to mankind; and God is faithful, so He will not allow you to be tempted beyond what you are able, but with the temptation will provide the way of escape also, so that you will be able to endure it.

The enemy is constantly scheming, but God has graciously given clear instructions on how to take a stand against those schemes. Proverbs 3:5–6 tells us:

> Trust in the LORD with all your heart
> And do not lean on your own understanding.
> In all your ways acknowledge Him,
> And He will make your paths straight.

We cannot succeed by simply trying harder or working smarter. Self-help efforts alone will always fail. The answer begins with surrender to the Holy Spirit.

### *4. Share the Harvest*

Trees produce their fruit to benefit others in two ways. For one, whether cultivated or in the wild, fruit is food, a source of nourishment for both people and wildlife.

Fruit also provides seeds for future harvests. As someone once observed, though you can easily count the seeds in an apple, it's impossible to count the apples in a seed. What a picture of how the Holy Spirit cultivates His fruit both to bless us and to make us a blessing to countless others!

As pastor, Bible teacher, and author Warren Wiersbe noted, "Fruit is produced to be eaten, not to be admired and put on display. . . . We do not bear fruit for our consumption; we bear fruit that others might be fed and helped, and that Christ might be glorified."[16] Bottom line: Cultivating the fruit of the Spirit is more about *we* than *me*.

In the following chapters we'll examine practical ways to share each of the nine facets of His fruit. We'll also explore ways to encourage others to nurture this fruit in their lives as, together, we yield to the Holy Spirit's leading.

Finally, at the end of each chapter, you will find questions for individual application or group discussion.

Ready? Let's reclaim what the enemy has attacked!

---

## APPLICATION QUESTIONS

1. Which of the nine displays of the fruit of the Spirit do you identify as particular strengths of yours?
2. In which of the nine displays of the fruit are you hoping for greater growth?
3. What does abiding in Christ look like in your life? How easy or difficult is it for you to consistently abide in Christ? Why?
4. How has the enemy tempted you to doubt God's Word regarding the fruit of the Spirit in your life?
5. How have you become vulnerable to the enemy's attacks through either pride or shame?
6. Which component(s) of the armor of God do you "put on" most consistently? Which do you put on less consistently?
7. How have you been trying to cultivate the Spirit's fruit in your own strength?
8. Which portion of the fourfold approach (recognize the enemy's tactics, nurture a right perspective, recover and grow, share the harvest) do you expect will provide the greatest surprises for you? Which do you anticipate will give the most familiar results?

CHAPTER 2

# The Heart of Our Fruit Is Love

Love is first on Paul's list of the Spirit's fruit in his letter to the Galatian church. Even though this fruit is ours by the Holy Spirit, we still struggle to love others the way God loves us. What's the problem?

## Recognize the Enemy's Tactics

Those squirrels in my backyard have a knack for picking the ripest mangoes before I can get to them. Again and again I've watched the fruit slowly ripen, only to be snatched before I harvest it. After repeated disappointments, I finally asked: Did the problem lie solely with the squirrels, or was I contributing to the situation?

The real problem wasn't the brazen bandits. They were just acting naturally. My own behavior made it easy for them—because I believed a lie. When a fruit appeared ready, I thought I could wait *one more day* for it to reach its juiciest peak. The squirrels used that lie to beat me to the prize almost every time.

Just as lies have a powerful impact on our natural experiences, they can also wreak havoc in our spiritual lives.

### *The Powerful Lie to Corrupt Our Love*

We've already seen our spiritual enemy described as the father of lies. Lies are his go-to strategy to attack the fruit of love that the Holy Spirit graciously nurtures in us. The enemy starts with one of the most powerful lies of all: *I must love others by trying harder.*

By putting all our effort into loving others better, we tell ourselves, we can make it happen. But we can't. Our efforts fail miserably. The lie that it's all on us actually makes it *more* difficult to love others. It corrupts our priorities and increases our discouragement.

Loving others cannot be our first priority. What should be? According to Jesus, it's this: "'You shall love the Lord your God with all your heart, and with all your soul, and with all your mind.' This is the great and foremost commandment. The second is like it, 'You shall love your neighbor as yourself'" (Matthew 22:37–39).

When we reverse the order of these commands, we will fail at loving others well. The devil knows this. And he leverages our vulnerability through distraction, entanglement, and desire for control.

### Distraction

Most Christians don't wake up one morning and decide, *Today I will stop loving God and others.* Neither does the enemy have the right to simply waltz in and steal our love while we're sleeping. Then where does our love go? The enemy's tactics are sneaky. He corrupts our priorities through distraction.

What distracts you from loving God with all your heart, soul, and mind? In his book *The Screwtape Letters*, C. S. Lewis describes the power of distraction in this fictional advice from a senior demon to a junior demon:

> You will find that anything or nothing is sufficient to attract his wandering attention. You no longer need a good book, which he really likes, to keep him from his prayers or his work or his sleep; a column of advertisements in yesterday's paper will do. . . . You can make him do nothing at all for long periods.[1]

What causes your attention and mine to be distracted from our first priority? To put it another way, what chokes our priority to love

God first? Jesus used a farming illustration to describe how the gospel message can be choked. We can also apply this parable to loving God: "The sower went out to sow; and as he sowed, some seeds . . . fell among the thorns, and the thorns came up and choked them out" (Matthew 13:3, 7).

Is the priority of loving God first being choked out of your life by thorns of lies?

Once we accept that first, foundational lie, *I must try harder,* our attitudes about love are easily influenced by two additional lies.

*I should love only those who deserve to be loved.* It seems reasonable to withhold our love from those we consider undeserving. Why waste our affection on them? The problem, however, is our unrealistic expectations. There will always be someone who lets us down, someone who fails to treat us as we believe we deserve. Aren't you glad God doesn't apply the same standard to us?

*I deserve to be treated better.* This lie is closely related to the first. Others aren't worthy, but we are—at least, so we think. We believe this lie because it strokes our ego. And we forget the admonition in Scripture not to think more highly of ourselves than we should.[2]

### Entanglement

Another of Satan's schemes: entangle us in sin.

Years ago I adopted two boxer puppies from the local humane society. Boxers are a highly active and playful breed. So playful, in fact, that when I walked the dogs, they often tangled me in their leashes as they ran circles around me. (My neighbors found this more amusing than I did.) All three of us remained stuck until I untangled my legs.

Sin has a similar effect. It leaves us tangled and stuck, unable to move forward physically, emotionally, and spiritually. This is why Hebrews 12:1 urges us to rid ourselves of "the sin which so easily entangles us."

Our failure to love God with all our hearts, souls, and minds flows from loving our own desires more. The enemy dangles those desires before us like proverbial carrots, and we start running, hoping that if we catch them they will make us happy. But they rarely do. Or if they do, it's only for a short time until another alluring carrot dangles and we're off and running again. And as we've already seen, if we're not loving God well, we'll never be able to love people well.

### *Desire for Control*

Closely related to the enemy's schemes to distract and entangle is our desire for control. The devil doesn't have to scheme very hard for this one because it's a natural tendency for us, especially when it comes to loving others.

*We* want to decide when a person merits our love. We want to dole out forgiveness when we think they deserve it. And we want to withhold love as a way of punishing those who hurt us.

Thankfully, God doesn't feel the same way. If anyone has a right to withhold love from the undeserving, it's Him. In light of the supreme sacrifice of His Son, God has the right to decide whom He wants to forgive, yet He freely offers His forgiveness and love to all who come. We excuse ourselves from following His example with words that have come from my own mouth much too often: "I'm not God. I'm only human!" How quickly the enemy wants us to forget God's goal as we surrender to His Holy Spirit: the goal of conforming us to the image of Christ.[3]

### *Our Contribution*

When we make loving God our priority, then our love for others becomes more than merely a warm affection for them in return for theirs for us. It is a sacrificial love. The lie of mistaking a shallower, transactional love for the real thing can keep us from offering the deep, genuine love that comes when we put God first. It's that second kind of love for others, so much higher than the first, that God calls us to—a love that flows not from our personal efforts but from the Holy Spirit, the source of love living in us.

## Nurture a Right Perspective

I love the taste of caramel. Sweet, chewy, creamy caramel. Add it to just about anything and I'm hooked. I'm not a big fan of coffee (don't hate me for that); however, my guilty pleasure is a frozen, blended caramel coffee, whether you call it a frappé or any other name. In reality, it's more of a coffee-flavored milkshake than a coffee. But hand me one of those and I'm all in.

I also love my family and friends. Some I've known for a lifetime; others I've met only in the past several months. In each case, our hearts are knit together through shared goals, interests, or experiences.

Finally, I'll always remember the feeling of being in love when I first met the man who would become my husband of forty years: an incomparable sense of excitement and anticipation while simultaneously feeling safe and protected.

### *Our Ways*

We think the same word for love applies to how we approach people and things. And that's part of a larger problem. We use just one English word, *love,* to translate several different words in the ancient Greek language.

The Greeks referred to erotic love, *eros,* as a love driven by sensual pleasure, including aspects of lust, passion, or romance. There's a place for eros within marriage, but if it's the only type of love, the marriage will ultimately fail as both people continually chase new objects of their passion.

Brotherly love, *philia,* describes a natural affection for those with shared interests and experiences or common goals. This conditional love will fail us when we face Jesus's command to love our enemies.[4]

*Storge* is familial love. Strong family ties provide a foundation from which we confidently venture into other relationships in all areas of life, including employment, friendships, and marriage. However, this type of love is limited to specific family circumstances.

The fourth type is *agapé,* an unconditional, sacrificial love rooted in the very nature of God. We'll discuss this in greater detail later in this chapter.

For now, the question is, When we talk about love, which type are we referring to?

Sensual love driven by physical attraction?

Reciprocal love focused on giving simply to get?

Loving another person solely because we're related to them?

Our culture tells us love is not worth the effort unless we get more than we give. However, being on the receiving end of such love often diminishes the relationship instead of enhancing it. I've interacted with people—maybe you have too—who clearly have a hidden agenda. Their actions and even their emotions are motivated by a goal I can only guess at. Who wants to remain in that kind of relationship?

Following the standards of love set by our culture doesn't work well. There's a better way.

## *God's Ways*

God wants us to know we're asking the wrong question. When we start by asking, "What is love?" our search will always lead us in the wrong direction. The first question to ask is "*Who* is love?" because love, first and foremost, is a Person. "God is love" (1 John 4:8). Love is not just something God does; it's who He *is*.

Not only is God love, His expressions of love began long before He created humanity. We know this from Jesus's prayer to His Father when He declared, "You loved Me before the foundation of the world" (John 17:24).

Author Bill Crowder describes it this way: "The Father and the Son have a shared love that is independent of creation, independent of humanity, independent of everything. . . . From all eternity past, there was never a moment without perfect, selfless love expressed between them."[5]

Only with the understanding of *who* love is can we ask *what* love is. What does it look like in you and me as we reflect the character of our heavenly Father? We find the answer in the apostle Paul's famous "love" passage in 1 Corinthians 13:4–8:

> Love is patient, love is kind, it is not jealous; love does not brag, it is not arrogant. It does not act disgracefully, it does not seek its own benefit; it is not provoked, does not keep an account of a wrong suffered, it does not rejoice in unrighteousness,

> but rejoices with the truth; it keeps every confidence, it believes all things, hopes all things, endures all things.
>
> Love never fails.

This love is not *eros, philia,* or *storge.* This is *agapé*: unconditional and sacrificial love with an eternal perspective that always seeks the other person's highest good. With the understanding that love is rooted in the very nature of God, Paul described what love is and what it is not.

If you were to ask me how I know I'm loved, I would describe my assurance using examples from my experiences: How my parents made sacrifices for me. How my husband consistently put my preferences above his own, whether in the choice of a movie, a restaurant, or the color of our carpets. It's easy for me to cite ways he demonstrated his love for me just about every day.

But if you were to ask me how I specifically show love to other people in my life, the answers don't come as readily. Perhaps that's because every person's needs are different. Or maybe it's because to love others well, I must first learn how to love God well.

Remember what Jesus said when asked about the most important commandment? Let's revisit His answer: "Love the Lord your God with all your heart, and with all your soul, and with all your mind" (Matthew 22:37). Sounds good, right? Now how do we live this out day by day?

### *Loving the Lord with All Your Heart*

This greatest command also results in the greatest gift. David wrote in Psalm 37:4: "Delight yourself in the LORD; and He will give you the desires of your heart." When we love the Lord with all our heart, He becomes our greatest delight. Our desires are rooted in Him. Our contentment is rooted in Him. And our hopes are rooted in Him. When the Lord is our greatest desire and greatest delight, our love for Him multiplies to fill the length and breadth of our deepest emotions.

### *Loving the Lord with All Your Soul*

Loving the Lord with all our soul touches the core of our identity. Who am I? My quick answer is that I am a child of God because I've trusted Christ as my Savior. That's the Sunday school answer. But what does it mean? Unless I understand my identity in Christ, I won't be able to love God and others well.

The apostle Paul's letter to the Ephesian church begins with a beautiful description of our identity. In Christ we are chosen, adopted, redeemed, forgiven, and recipients of God's abundant grace.[6] And that's just from the first few verses.

Knowing who we are in Christ causes a spring of love and gratitude to overflow in our hearts for the one who offers salvation freely to us at great cost to Himself. How can I not deeply love the Father who first loved me? And how can I not also love others with the love He has lavished on me?

### *Loving the Lord with All Your Mind*

Have you ever heard the criticism that to become a Christian, you have to "check your brain at the door"? Or that belief in Christ requires "blind faith"? The implication is that intelligent people couldn't possibly believe in God, Jesus, the Bible, or anything else related to Christianity.

Yet throughout history physicists, biologists, inventors, kings, statesmen, and other brilliant people from all walks of life have examined Scripture and found a credible biblical worldview. Archaeological discoveries continue to support the biblical record. History, accompanied by our personal experiences, affirms the claims of Scripture. We can freely love the Lord with all our minds as well as all our hearts and souls.

The Bible reminds us to set our minds on the things of the Spirit,[7] renew our minds,[8] and take every thought captive in obedience to Christ.[9] We're reminded to focus our thoughts on what is true, honorable, right, pure, lovely, and commendable.[10] And, of course, to love the Lord with all our minds.[11]

Author John Musyimi notes, “Deep Christian affection and devotion is inextricably tied to treasured biblical truths you believe with all your mind.”[12] Loving the Lord with our minds involves reading His Word, not just to skim it or check a box on our to-do list, but to study it for the purpose of transformation. What begins in our minds changes our hearts and flows out to our behavior.

## Recover and Grow

Gardening is therapeutic for me. After spending hours writing on my laptop, I welcome the physical activity of weeding, pruning, and planting. However, sometimes gardening can be more of a battle than a simple activity. Last year, as I worked in an overlooked corner of my yard, I discovered a six-foot-tall shrub smothered under a blanket of kudzu. Kudzu is an invasive perennial vine common in the southern states. When mature, it can cover a host shrub or tree in just a few weeks.

Conquering the kudzu vine required attacking it on two fronts. First, I ripped out the clinging tendrils choking the shrub’s branches, even though I removed the few remaining healthy leaves in the process. Then I uprooted the vine to prevent facing the same battle again. Sadly, the shrub was so damaged that I had to prune its bare branches to a foot or two off the ground. I hoped it would survive not just the attack but also the cure.

Satan’s tactics often have a similar effect on our ability to love well. As we’ve seen, the Holy Spirit’s fruit of love can be choked through lies, distractions, and sin. So how can we apply what we’ve learned to recover what the thief has attacked and cultivate new growth instead?

We start by refuting lies with truth—truth about the *source* of love, the *priority* of love, the *holiness* of love, and *how* to love.

### *Surrendering to the Source of Love*

A key Bible verse about love tells us, “We love, because He first loved us” (1 John 4:19). Most Christians easily acknowledge this intellectually and spiritually without realizing we respond to this truth emotionally, as well.

Do you believe God loves you? You! I'm not talking about a John 3:16 kind of love: "For God so loved the world . . ." I'm talking about a Song of Solomon 2:13 love. The personal, intimate kind of love that declares, "Arise, my darling, my beautiful one, and come along!" Is this what you hear God saying to you when you open His Word? Is it *why* you open His Word? Or do you read and study God's Word because that's what good Christians are supposed to do?

Paul wrote to the Corinthian church, "I am jealous for you with a godly jealousy. I promised you to one husband, to Christ" (2 Corinthians 11:2 NIV). Our faith in Christ places us in the position of being His bride. Do you recognize the voice of Christ saying specifically to *you*, "Arise, my darling, and come"?

Satan doesn't want us to feel God's intimate, personal love. Instead, the devil entices us to view God's love from a distance. When we do, our love for Him and for others will also be offered from a distance.

### *Committing to the Priority of Love*

We've seen that we can't love others by trying harder if loving the Lord is not our first priority. So how do we love the Lord with all our hearts, souls, and minds?

In *Loving God with All My Heart*, Julie Ackerman Link observed, "Loving God with all our hearts means desiring God as He desires us; it means having the relationship with God that He desires to have with us."[13]

We say we want intimacy with God more than anything else—until God's sovereignty allows situations in our life that don't fit our plans. Then we hold back—just a bit—because we're afraid to trust Him fully. Is our whole heart surrendered to His plans, or are we holding tightly to our own agendas?

Jesus spoke about the focus of our hearts when He said this in Matthew 6:19–21:

> Do not store up for yourselves treasures on earth, where moth and rust destroy, and where thieves break in and steal. But store up for yourselves treasures in heaven, where neither moth nor

> rust destroys, and where thieves do not break in or steal; for where your treasure is, there your heart will be also.

If loving God fully—no holding back—means wanting for ourselves what *He* wants for us, then we will trust Him fully. And we'll do it with our whole heart because He loved us first.

### *Pursuing the Holiness of Love*

Our identity is in Christ and our love for God will flow from that identity. And because we are children of God, we will live as children of God. He chose us to be holy, and in love He adopted us into His family through Jesus Christ.[14]

We don't often associate holiness with love. But Jesus said if we love Him, we will obey Him.[15] We can't do so by relying only on our own efforts, though. The Spirit of Christ is the one who transforms us to be more like Him as we surrender to His work in our lives. Theologian and author J. I. Packer wrote, "The heart of holiness is the spirit of love."[16] The Holy Spirit is both the source of the fruit of love and the one who makes us holy.

Strangely, though, we rarely connect love to the Holy Spirit even when we refer to *agapé*. We speak of the love of the Father and the love Jesus has for us—a love that paid for our sins on the cross. Yet for the believer, our ability to love deeply and genuinely directly connects to the indwelling of the Holy Spirit, the third person of the Trinity. The resulting fruit begins with nurturing the gift of love. The other eight characteristics flow from this wellspring. It's no surprise, then, that our spiritual enemy is determined to corrupt this fruit in God's children.

### *Being Intentional About How We Love*

Love is a choice of the will. But we can bend our will in the wrong direction. Instead of loving intentionally, too often we determine who we *won't* love.

There's something deceptively freeing about deciding who deserves to be loved by us. But that's not how God loves. If it were, none of us would be recipients of His love. We *have* received His love, though, which enables us to love Him back. If God did not love us first, we would not have the capacity to love Him at all.

This leads to an uncomfortable truth. If we claim to love God, we are obligated to love each other. Jon Bloom, cofounder of the Desiring God website, noted, "Our love for each other is an indicator of the place God is holding in our hearts."[17]

So as we commit to reflecting our love for God by loving others, let's lay aside any thoughts of withholding our love from those who seem unworthy. That's about control—but the control we *think* we have is just an illusion that we have the right to love the worthy and punish the unworthy. That isn't *agapé*. Real love doesn't come from us. It originates with the Holy Spirit. Love is His gift to us.

By the way, just in case you're wondering whether my shrub survived the kudzu attack, it now thrives with healthy new growth!

## Share the Harvest

Country music star Reba McEntire released a song titled "Love Isn't Love 'Til You Give It Away." The song's message reminds me of a Bible verse that instructs followers of Christ to be doers of God's Word and not just hearers of His Word.[18]

Our motivation to love isn't something we force because that's what Christians should do. Rather, our motivation to love others flows from knowing we are loved by God. Oswald Chambers observed, "The knowledge that God has loved me beyond all limits will compel me to go into the world to love others in the same way."[19]

### *Show Me*

Remember the conversation Jesus had with Peter in John 21:15–17?

> When they had finished breakfast, Jesus said to Simon Peter, "Simon, son of John, do you love Me more than these?" He said to Him, "Yes, Lord; You know that I love You." He said to him, "Tend My lambs." He said to him again, a second time, "Simon, son of John, do you love Me?" He said to Him, "Yes,

> Lord; You know that I love You." He said to him, "Shepherd My sheep." He said to him the third time, "Simon, son of John, do you love Me?" Peter was hurt because He said to him the third time, "Do you love Me?" And he said to Him, "Lord, You know all things; You know that I love You." Jesus said to him, "Tend My sheep."

After Jesus's resurrection, He repeatedly asked Peter, "Do you love Me?" A multitude of books and sermons have been written explaining the importance of the threefold repetition of this question, along with exploring the two different Greek words for love in this passage.

Notice Jesus's response *after* Peter answered each of the repeated questions. Three times, Jesus followed Peter's answer with a command to *do* something. "Tend My lambs . . . Shepherd My sheep . . . Tend My sheep."

In other words, don't just *tell* me you love me. *Show* me you love me. And as a friend recently reminded me, Jesus did *not* tell Peter he had to *like* the sheep. He just had to serve them!

Jesus expects us to love others. I'll be the first to admit this can be easier said than done. It's even more difficult when we consider that not just any love is good enough. Nope. God calls us to love with His love: *agapé*.

The second greatest commandment is to love our neighbor as we love ourselves.[20] So who is our neighbor? In Luke 10:30–35, Jesus answered this question with the parable of the Good Samaritan:

> A man was going down from Jerusalem to Jericho, and he encountered robbers, and they stripped him and beat him, and went away leaving him half dead. And by coincidence a priest was going down on that road, and when he saw him, he passed by on the other side. Likewise a Levite also, when he came to the place and saw him, passed by on the other side. But a Samaritan who was on a journey came upon him; and when he saw him, he felt compassion, and came to him and bandaged

> up his wounds, pouring oil and wine on them; and he put him on his own animal, and brought him to an inn and took care of him. On the next day he took out two denarii and gave them to the innkeeper and said, "Take care of him; and whatever more you spend, when I return, I will repay you."

This parable illustrates two key points about loving others: *whom* to love and *how* to love. Who is our neighbor? Anyone the Lord allows in our life. Not just the people who share our lifestyles or interests. In this passage, a Samaritan cared for someone who would have despised him because of his identity. And the care he offered rose beyond minimal assistance or convenience. The Samaritan offered the kind of love and care he would have wanted extended to himself if he were in the same situation.

Author Joseph Stowell reminds us:

> It doesn't make any difference if you like them or not; if they deserve your attention or not; if your attention to them is rewarded or not; or even if they misunderstand and respond to your care in negative ways. . . . All of that is totally irrelevant. . . . You aren't doing it for them. You are doing it for Jesus, who does deserve all the love you can muster.[21]

### *A New Source*

Have you ever watched a television program about hoarders? Hoarders are people who have a compulsion to excessively save all their possessions. They are unable to discard anything for fear they will need it someday. Because of this disorder, they become prisoners of their compulsion, unable to function in healthy relationships.

When we fail to love others as God loves us, we are in effect hoarding His love. Put another way, we become like the Dead Sea, which takes in water from the Jordan River but has no outlet. As a result, it cannot support life because of its high salt content.

While we may not consciously hoard the love we receive, we can make excuses to rationalize why we love some people and not others.

After all, some people are just not lovable! But loving the lovable is easy. Loving the unlovable? Not so much. It can become easier, however, when we ask the Holy Spirit to let us see others from His perspective.

I speak from personal experience. When one family member betrayed the trust of another, my husband and I struggled with how to respond. Even after the perpetrator expressed regret for their actions, I maintained a cool civility in their presence. Still, I knew this wasn't enough. So I asked God to allow me to see this person as He saw them. As time passed, the Holy Spirit gave me greater insight into their brokenness. It's important to note that loving this person did not mean I condoned their actions, just as God's love for me does not indicate support of my sin. Love also did not mean I trusted them. If trust were to redevelop, it would require time within the boundaries of a healthy relationship.

Still, I knew God was calling me to allow Him to love that person through me. Impossible if I were the source of this love. Possible, though, when I remember this love flows from a source *other* than me.

In John 15:5, Jesus told His disciples that their ability to bear fruit depended on their connection to Him: "I am the vine, you are the branches; the one who remains in Me, and I in him bears much fruit, for apart from Me you can do nothing."

This relationship is critical because Jesus was about to give them a command that would be impossible to obey apart from utter dependence on Him. Seven verses later, in verse 12, He commanded them, "Love one another, just as I have loved you." Remember who He was talking to: a tax collector and a zealot; an uneducated fisherman in Jesus's inner circle and an educated money-handler who betrayed Him; and one called "beloved" along with one labeled "doubter." They were all to set aside preconceived perceptions in order to love each other as Jesus loved them. Natural ability to love, apart from the power of the Holy Spirit, would have been woefully inadequate. No wonder Jesus knew this needed to be a command instead of a suggestion!

## *Extraordinary Characteristics*

It's not a coincidence that love is listed first among the fruit of the Spirit, for the other eight displays of the Holy Spirit's fruit all flow from a fountain of love. As we saw in 1 Corinthians 13:4–8 (NIV), Paul described the extraordinary characteristics of love. Let's look at them one more time:

> Love is patient, love is kind. It does not envy, it does not boast, it is not proud. It does not dishonor others, it is not self-seeking, it is not easily angered, it keeps no record of wrongs. Love does not delight in evil but rejoices with the truth. It always protects, always trusts, always hopes, always perseveres.
>
> Love never fails.

We often hear this familiar passage read at weddings and anniversary celebrations. It sets a high standard, one that seeks God's ultimate best for the other person. The cost of such love requires setting aside our own interests and preferences. As author and speaker Elisabeth Elliot wrote, "To aim at loving instead of at being loved requires sacrifice. Love reaches out, willing to be turned down or inconvenienced, expecting no personal reward, wanting only to give."[22] Isn't this what Jesus did for us? And if He loves us this way, what excuse do we have for not loving others in the same way?[23]

We may not ever be in a position to die for someone else as Jesus gave His life for us. However, we can give of our time or material resources. We can listen and encourage. We can show care and compassion. And we can walk in forgiveness. In the course of these acts of love, we'll find we are, indeed, dying to self as we love those around us.

When we love God first, with all our hearts, souls, and minds, Satan loses the ability to attack what God cultivates in us by His Spirit. Still, if the devil fails here, he doesn't give up. Satan's next step is to prevent us from loving anyone else with this same love, because he knows what the apostle John tells us: If we don't love those we can see, then we don't really love God. "The one who loves God must also love his brother and sister" (1 John 4:21).

Our ability to love the Lord before we love others comes from God Himself. We love Him and others *because* He first loved us. And while loving the Lord must be our priority, it's also just the beginning.

Loving God first means surrendering to His plans, purposes, goals, and desires for us, not because we have to but because we want to. As we abide in Christ—connected to Him as a branch connects to a tree trunk—we can then love others as God loves us.

John wrote in 1 John 4:7–8, "Beloved, let's love one another; for love is from God, and everyone who loves has been born of God and knows God. The one who does not love does not know God, because God is love." My personal translation and summary of those two verses?

God *is* love, God *gives* love, and God *equips* us to love.

---

## APPLICATION QUESTIONS

1. In what relationship have you tried harder to love the other person without success? Why did trying harder fail?
2. When have you been tempted to withhold love from someone you determined to be undeserving? How does this compare with God's love for you?
3. When have you been tempted to withhold love from someone who did not treat you the way you thought you should be treated?
4. How does knowing that God not only is loving but is *love* help you understand the nature of *agapé*?
5. During a typical day, what does loving the Lord with all your heart look like? Loving the Lord with all your soul? Loving the Lord with all your mind?
6. How does knowing your identity in Christ enable you to love well?
7. What does it mean to surrender to God in order to love better?
8. If our ability to love others indicates our love for God, how satisfied are you with your level of love for God and others?
9. How was the Good Samaritan's love extravagant? What holds

you back from loving extravagantly? (Note: Extravagant love is not limited to financial extravagance.)

10. Which "neighbor" is God calling you to love in practical ways? How will you love that person this week?

CHAPTER 3

# The Song of Our Fruit Is Joy

What diminishes your joy? Most of us can readily list situations and people we label as joy stealers. But did you know being joyful is not a suggestion? It's a command, regardless of our circumstances. In a letter to the Thessalonian church, the apostle Paul told his readers to "rejoice always" (1 Thessalonians 5:16). Yet in our broken, sin-sick world, the ability to always rejoice can sometimes seem impossible.

## Recognize the Enemy's Tactics

The Bible tells us Satan is the god of this world.[1] So it should be no surprise that he uses the troubles of this world to target the Spirit's fruit in our lives. Since the joy of the Lord is our refuge,[2] the devil does not hesitate to use whatever worldly weapons are at his disposal to attack the source of our protection and strength. And, as usual, he does not fight fair.

My friends Frank and Laura are experiencing the effects of living with incapacitating pain as I write this chapter. Chronic back pain drove Frank to undergo several surgeries over a period of years, with surgeons promising relief each time. Not only did the surgeries fail to deliver, but his debilitating pain increased exponentially. This Christian couple who have served their Savior most of their lives are now surrounded by loved ones asking, "Why? What is the purpose of this incessant, soul-crushing pain?" Joy erodes bit by bit each day even as these steadfast followers of Christ continue to cling to the Lord in faith.

We yearn for purpose. The devil knows this all too well. And because Satan is the father of lies, he uses our circumstances to lead us to despair. *What's the point?* he whispers. *Life is nothing more than a series of random, meaningless events.*

"What's the point?" is a question we're prone to ask with greater frequency in a world that appears increasingly purposeless. Whether during a life-altering event or a boring business meeting, we long to know: What is being accomplished?

And so we fall for another lie: There is no purpose to life.

This lie begins with the theory that the universe just happened and life came into existence through random chemical combinations that evolved into living organisms. The lie grows as we buy into the supposition that humanity is just a higher rung of the evolutionary ladder.

The foundation of Satan's strategy is to make us believe life has no purpose. If we accept that, then our joy is at best fragile, and diminishing it becomes as easy as taking a breath.

## The Thief's Methods

Once this wrong foundation is established, everything we build our joy upon becomes unstable. Hopelessness invades purposeless lives through a variety of ways.

*Suffering.* Pain is the great equalizer. Regardless of our economic status, national origin, or age, we all instinctively avoid suffering. When it occurs, then unless we see a greater purpose, either we try to run from it or we fall into a black hole of hopelessness. The temporal overpowers our eternal perspective as physical pain becomes all-consuming. In a world where comfort is extolled as the supreme goal, anything less cultivates despair.

A story is told of a professor who held a glass of water in front of his class and asked his students, "How heavy is this glass?" Based on the size of the glass and the amount of water it held, the students' guesses ranged from eight to sixteen ounces. But they missed the professor's point. The answer wasn't numerical. The glass would become heavier the longer he held it. A minute? No big deal. An hour? Uncomfortable. A day? . . . What begins with ease shifts to discomfort and then to pain. It isn't the weight but the duration of carrying it that makes the difference.

Over time, unrelenting suffering can strip our joy.

*Discontentment.* One of the quickest ways I can lose my joy is through comparison—what I call the "I wish" trap.

> *I wish I had her car instead of driving my old clunker.*
> *I wish I had his money to travel like he does.*
> *I wish I could sing like the worship leader at church.*
> *I wish . . .*

The more I wish, the more I compare, and the more I want what someone else has. When I focus on what I don't have, not only does my contentment fade but my joy fades with it.

Does it seem strange that in God's commandments, He names coveting and murder as equally unacceptable?[3] Satan knows the real issue is not necessarily the object of our desire. The real issue is that when we focus on what we don't have, we're not satisfied with what God has given us—and we want to correct what we see as His mistake.

*Habitual sin.* Ongoing sin can be demoralizing. Whether it's a hidden attitude or a specific behavior, habitual sin confines us to cycles of failure as we suffocate under a blanket of defeat. Even knowing our purpose can seem pointless when a habit becomes a barrier to intimacy with the Father. The devil doesn't need to expend additional energy as we fall prey to the trap of our own sin. We adopt an identity of victimhood. After all, if I haven't been able to uproot this sin in my life, I might as well give up. We cry with the apostle Paul, "For the good that I want, I do not do, but I practice the very evil that I do not want. . . . Who will set me free . . . ?" (Romans 7:19, 24).

*Doubting our salvation.* Suffering and habitual sin can also lead to another tactic used by Satan to spoil our joy: doubting our salvation. We wonder, *Is this level of suffering an indication that I've lost the protection that comes from being a child of God?* Or, *If I can't conquer this sin, does that mean I have not truly experienced salvation?*

Doubting our salvation causes us to fall into the trap of thinking that once saved by grace, remaining in that position depends on our efforts. Joy disappears in a haze of exhausting labor to somehow prove to God we're worthy of His salvation.

*Misplaced priorities.* While sin can block our understanding of our purpose, good works can too. Who would have thought the devil would encourage Christians to be busy for God? But those who say yes to a dozen different ministries can become spread so thin they lose sight of God's purpose for them. They're like a circus performer spinning plates on poles, desperately racing from one plate to the next to keep them all going at once. The performer can never commit to any one plate for fear the others will come crashing down.

*Wrong motives.* Then there's the Christian who attends church every week and has a quiet time in God's Word daily because that's what "good Christians" do. They go through the motions. Obligation, not joyful devotion, becomes their motive: something they *have* to do instead of something they *get* to do.

Or perhaps they're driven by a desire for approval or admiration. Either way, the enemy sits back and gloats when behavior meant to draw us into a joyful relationship with God instead drains our joy.

*Grief.* An exploration of the enemy's tactics for diminishing our joy would not be complete without considering grief. Satan seeks to manipulate natural grief over our losses into obsessive grief, causing us to forget this world is not our home. Our temporary, physical lives become all-consuming black holes. We focus on whom we've lost to the exclusion of all else.

Did you see yourself—even a little—in any of these descriptions? We can excuse our discouragement as being due to a temporary season, a recent hurt, or the lure of temptation. Still, temporary seasons have a way of transforming into lifelong ruts that keep us trapped. Our understandings of the purpose for which we were created get corrupted, and so we lose the fruit of joy. The first step in our recovery is to explore the relationship between purpose and joy from God's perspective.

## Nurture a Right Perspective

When I was an adolescent, I attended a church youth group where the leader taught a lesson on the distinction between joy and happiness: "Happiness is found in happenings; joy is found in Jesus." I struggled with this for years afterward because, to a child, what's the difference? Jesus "happened" two thousand years ago, and while I believed in Him, how was that different from the pleasure of doing the things I enjoyed?

### *Our Ways*

We think joy is only found in pleasure. And what produces pleasure will differ for each person. Those sources of pleasure are usually external: people, places, and possessions. We chase temporary experiences and relationships, or we pour ourselves into work or even into ministry, searching for purpose and happiness. When we think we've found what we're craving, we learn this happiness is as fleeting as fog that dissipates at sunrise. So we start all over again. Our lives resemble a hamster on a wheel, constantly running from one person to the next and one thrill to the next. We end up back where we started and wonder, *Is this really the best that life can be? Will lasting joy always be just beyond my grasp until I finally reach heaven?*

### *God's Ways*

God wants us to know that lasting joy is possible in this life. The trouble is, we frequently miss the key to unlocking the abundant life that flows from this fruit of the Spirit. And that key is *not* found in our response to our circumstances.

Before the days of routine digital transactions, breakfast cereal boxes often touted appealing offers aimed at children. In exchange for mailing a certain number of box tops, kids could request membership in a secret club, complete with an official membership card and secret decoder ring. The unimpressive, plastic ring promised to unlock secret messages, which, as you may have guessed, would be found on future cereal boxes. This genius marketing ploy kept kids clamoring for that particular brand of cereal, guaranteeing parents would buy it week after week.

Today we're bombarded with adult versions of the secret decoder ring, especially when it comes to regaining joy. Buy a book, attend a Bible study, listen to a speaker, pray more, follow these five steps (or three, or ten), and your joy will return.

From the perspective of God's Word, we've got it backward. Joy is *not* sourced in something we do. And the answer is not a secret, although we often skip right past it, regardless of how many times we've read Zephaniah 3:17:

> The LORD your God is in your midst,
> A victorious warrior.
> He will rejoice over you with joy,
> He will be quiet in His love,
> He will rejoice over you with shouts of joy.

When we think of God's attributes, words such as *holy*, *just*, *righteous*, *compassionate*, and *merciful* easily come to mind. But *joyous*? Yes, joy describes God too!

The Lord, the creator of the universe, rejoices over those who belong to Him. While these words were written to ancient Israel, how could we imagine, even for a moment, that He rejoices over us any less—we who have been purchased with the blood of His Son?

Our joy begins with God's joy for us. Sounds simple, doesn't it? Then what's the problem? Is it possible the problem is rooted in how we define the source of our purpose?

### *Back to Purpose*

"Which came first, the chicken or the egg?"

People puzzled over this riddle for ages. Some secular biologists asserted the egg came first; those who believe the biblical account of creation maintained the chicken came first. However, scientific research recently concluded the development of an eggshell requires a particular protein found only in the ovaries of a chicken.[4] God created chickens, which in turn lay eggs. What does this have to do with joy? It's all about what we believe is the source of our purpose and joy.

My tendency toward a type A personality has consistently caused me to associate purpose with activity—as if I could manufacture joy. Understanding God's purpose for my life began with identifying how to serve Him. While He has prepared good works for me to do,[5] I had the order wrong. Our purpose does not begin with service.

Instead, our truest purpose is birthed from an intimate relationship with the one who created us for fellowship with Himself. That fellowship had been broken by sin and required restoration beyond our ability to repair. So God, who rejoices over us, did what we could not do for ourselves. He restored our relationship with Him.

The purpose—and therefore joy—of every Christian *always* begins with this relationship. Serving God isn't a bad desire. But when we prioritize serving Him over intimacy with Him, we fall into the same joyless trap as the Pharisees did in Jesus's day. The apostle Paul intentionally established the order of relationship and service in Ephesians 2:

> For by grace you have been saved through faith; and this is not of yourselves, it is the gift of God; not a result of works, so that no one may boast. (vv. 8–9)
>
> We are His workmanship, created in Christ Jesus for good works, which God prepared beforehand so that we would walk in them. (v. 10)

Which comes first? The order of these verses makes it clear. The gift of a restored relationship with the Father is the source from which our service flows, and therefore, is the source of our joy.

We see this illustrated after Jesus's seventy-two followers returned from their mini mission trip. Gospel writer Luke noted they "returned with joy" as they shared how even the demons submitted to them in Jesus's name (Luke 10:17). While Jesus was pleased with the fruit of their travels, He also gave them a gentle rebuke: "Do not rejoice in this, that the spirits are subject to you, but rejoice that your names are recorded in heaven" (v. 20). Once again, the source of eternal joy is first found in a relationship with the Lord!

Sadly, we often view eternal life and eternal joy as something we have to wait for. We struggle under the circumstances of this earthly life. *Someday, when this life is over and eternal life begins, I'll finally experience true joy.* Jesus revealed the error of this perspective: "The one who hears My word, and believes Him who sent Me, has eternal life, and does not come into judgment, but has passed out of death into life" (John 5:24).

For much of my adult life, I totally missed the present tense of this verse. He did not say, "*will* have eternal life"; He said, "*has* eternal life." Joy springing from eternal life is something we can have *now*. We can echo Psalm 71:23:

> My lips will shout for joy when I sing praises to You;
> And my soul, which You have redeemed.

## What About Suffering?

You might be thinking, *I agree that a restored relationship with God is both our ultimate purpose and our source of joy. But what about suffering? Isn't it naive to ignore the effects of suffering on our ability to be joyful?*

The experience of the apostles paints a different picture. In Acts 5, after fearlessly preaching the gospel, they were arrested and forced to stand trial before the Sanhedrin, the Jewish supreme court. These first

Christians were beaten and ordered "not to speak in the name of Jesus" (Acts 5:40). How did they respond? "They went on their way from the presence of the Council, rejoicing that they had been considered worthy to suffer shame for His name" (v. 41).

In case we might think this ability to rejoice in the midst of suffering was limited to the apostles, in 1 Peter 1:6–8, Peter wrote these words which have been an encouragement to believers throughout history:

> In this you *greatly rejoice*, even though now for a little while, if necessary, you have been distressed by various trials, so that the proof of your faith, being more precious than gold which perishes though tested by fire, may be found to result in praise, glory, and honor at the revelation of Jesus Christ; and though you have not seen Him, you love Him, and though you do not see Him now, but believe in Him, you *greatly rejoice* with joy inexpressible and full of glory.

Or consider James's message to believers: "Consider it all joy, my brothers and sisters, when you encounter various trials, knowing that the testing of your faith produces endurance" (James 1:2–3).

I'll be the first to admit, these verses appear contrary to common sense. We don't expect rejoicing to follow suffering or joy to follow trials. But is this because such joy doesn't make sense or because we've believed a lie for so long that it masquerades as truth? Now that we know the truth, how do we combat the lie and recover our joy?

## Recover and Grow

I began this chapter with an example of how unrelenting pain can lead to despair when the purpose seems nonexistent. Allow me to share a similar situation with a different outcome.

Russ spent most of our forty-year marriage as a nominal Christian. Some have described this as the "eighteen-inch difference"—the distance between the head and the heart. He was a kind and gentle person. Yet for a variety of reasons, he had never received Christ as his personal Savior. Until pain changed everything. A visit to the emergency room revealed a tumor. Further testing exposed pancreatic cancer.

I entered the hospital room the morning after his surgery to discover a changed person. His first words? "I have to tell you something. Even if I don't leave this hospital bed alive, it's okay. God has given me the most important healing I could ask for."

The Holy Spirit had met him right where he was, bringing new spiritual life. Over the next year, Russ's pain increased tremendously as the cancer spread. Still, he spent his final months sharing the singular message the Lord planted in his soul: "Even if God does not heal this cancer, He has healed my heart and my mind, and that's much more important than healing my body. God is in control. Trust Him for the peace and joy only He can give regardless of your situation. I'm living proof despite my prognosis of terminal cancer."

Russ found his purpose—and his joy—in vibrant new life even as he faced death.

God has recently been teaching me a challenging lesson: to surrender to His sovereignty. Even more specifically, to release my need to know *why*. Because the reality is, we don't always have the privilege of understanding the purpose of every trying situation. If recovering our joy depends on God explaining why He allows difficult situations, then we would all be consigned to joyless lives. Consider the book of Job in the Old Testament. Even in the end, the Lord never did tell Job the reason He allowed the depth of Job's suffering. Still, God was with him through it all.

## *No Greater Joy*

Have you ever felt you would explode if you did not break into praise to the God of our salvation? Paul did this in several places in his New Testament letters. It's as if he couldn't help himself. For example, after explaining the future salvation of the Gentiles along with God's chosen people, Paul broke into a doxology—a song of praise—in Romans 11:33–36:

> Oh, the depth of the riches, both of the wisdom and knowledge of God! How unsearchable are His judgments and unfathomable His ways! For who has known the mind of the Lord, or who became His counselor? Or who has first given to Him, that it would be paid back to him? For from Him, and through Him, and to Him are all things. To Him be the glory forever. Amen.

Paul's uncontainable joy sprang from his understanding of God's plan of salvation for all people, Jews *and* Gentiles. There is no greater joy than knowing our ultimate purpose has been fulfilled: the purpose of being reconciled to our Creator. And our ability to joyfully glorify God flows from that restored relationship.

In Paul's letter to the Philippian believers, he repeatedly referenced joy despite writing from a prison cell. Even though rivals appeared determined to show Paul up, he could still say in Philippians 1:18, "What does it matter? The important thing is that in every way, whether from false motives or true, Christ is preached. And because of this I rejoice. Yes, and I will continue to rejoice" (NIV).

What an example for us! We may say we're confident God is always at work for our ultimate good and His eternal glory. Yet the true test of our confidence is our level of joy when life does *not* work out the way we want.

Some might label this spiritual hypocrisy—a way of saying we're to "fake it till we make it." God is not advocating hypocrisy. Rather, we're called to respond to the facts of who God is rather than rely on momentary emotions. The Holy Spirit then releases joy based on those facts rather than on our feelings. Still, it's one thing to talk about this in theory and quite another to live it out daily.

### *Practicing Joy in Practical Ways*

The devil may work to use circumstances to cheat us out of our joy in Christ. But notice in Paul's letter to the Philippian church, he wrote that we are to "rejoice in the Lord always" (Philippians 4:4). Once again, this is a command—not a suggestion—to be intentional about surrendering to the Holy Spirit, rejoicing in Him. Joy is a choice of the will, finding its source in God Himself instead of dependence on our situation. How do we do that? How can we confront each of the enemy's strategies to spoil our joy, and use them as stepping stones to the very joy he works to sabotage?

## *Steering Through Suffering*

Encouragement to be joyful in suffering can come across as shallow clichés. The words may be true, but they can often seem dismissive of our pain. That is, unless we train our focus away from the cause and shift to the result.

In our broken world, suffering is not merely a possibility, it's a probability. However, my greatest times of spiritual growth and intimacy with the Lord blossomed from seasons of suffering. I wish my greatest spiritual growth flowed from times of ease, health, and pleasure. Instead, God grows me in reliance on Him especially in seasons of suffering, in ways pleasure can never produce.

The Lord also uses my suffering to equip me to comfort someone else. There's a tongue twister in 2 Corinthians 1:3–4 that says, "Blessed be the God and Father of our Lord Jesus Christ, the Father of mercies and God of all comfort, who comforts us in all our affliction so that we will be able to comfort those who are in any affliction with the comfort with which we ourselves are comforted by God." Whew, that's a mouthful! The truth is, God may use my seasons of suffering more for someone else than for me.

## *Silencing the "I Wish" of Discontentment*

How much is enough? Enough talent, enough possessions, enough money? And who decides how much is enough? The more we compare, the more unhappy we become.

If we're not careful, discontentment can not only decrease our joy but also hinder our intimacy with God. Discontentment can move us from "I want" to "Why is God keeping something good from me?" There's no better place to help correct this thinking than the pages of Genesis 3. In desiring the forbidden fruit, Adam and Eve failed to rejoice in the countless fruit trees in the garden. Instead, they lost their joy by focusing on the fruit of the one tree they could not have. And the ramifications of their wrong thinking have reverberated throughout human history.

### *Standing Against Temptation*

*Sanctification* is not a word that often appears in our conversations. To be sanctified is to be set apart or made holy as God's people. But we're not the ones who do the setting apart. God does. He is the one who told the ancient Israelites, "I am the Lord who sanctifies you" (Leviticus 22:32). And in 1 Thessalonians 5:23 we read, "May the God of peace Himself sanctify you."

One of the most difficult lessons I needed to learn about habitual sin is that trying harder is not the solution. Of course we need to do our part to stand against temptation. However, our victories—and our joy—come from surrendering to the Holy Spirit who does the work in us. As with other facets of the fruit of the Spirit, the answer is not just to try harder. The answer starts with surrender.

### *Sealing Our Salvation*

Oh, how the enemy loves to sap our joy by causing us to doubt our salvation! We forget we did nothing to earn our salvation, therefore we can do nothing to lose our salvation. The apostle Paul reminded believers that our salvation is a gift to us by God's grace through Jesus Christ.[6]

The apostle John echoed that truth: "These things I have written to you who believe in the name of the Son of God, so that you may know that you have eternal life" (1 John 5:13). Not that we might *hope* we have a restored relationship with God but that we might *know* we have it.

### *Shifting Our Priorities*

There's a reason we're called human beings, not human doings. Our sense of purpose and subsequent joy is rooted first in a restored relationship with our heavenly Father. Sadly, as we've already noted, the accompanying joy is easily crowded out by busyness. Does God want our service? Yes. But not when we prioritize service over relationship.

Jude's opening greeting in his New Testament letter highlights the importance of relationship. He addressed his letter "To those who have been called, who are loved in God the Father and kept for Jesus Christ" (Jude v. 1 NIV). Notice he did not refer to their service for God in this opening verse. They were first referred to as called, loved, and kept. Appeals regarding their service were included in the verses that followed.

### *Searching Our Motives*

Some mornings I awake with my to-do list circling my thoughts the way water circles a drain before it disappears. Tasks weigh on me, sapping my joy. I have to go to church because that's what good Christians do. I have to give my time and finances because that's what's expected of church members. I have to read my Bible and spend time in prayer because those are the disciplines of the Christian life.

However, everything changes when I reexamine each have-to, shifting it to a want-to and then to a get-to. From drudgery to enjoyment to privilege. For example:

> I *have to* trust God because I have no other options,
> shifts to
> I *want to* trust God because He has always been faithful,
> and then to
> I *get to* trust the God of the universe because He loves me and saved me.

Or how about Bible reading:

> I *have to* read the Bible because that's what Christians do,
> shifts to
> I *want to* read the Bible because it is spiritually nutritious,
> and then to
> I *get to* read the Bible because its sweetness blesses my spirit.

So the next time a have-to saps your joy, consider how the Lord wants to change it to a want-to and then a get-to!

### *Steadying Our Grief*

Seasons of grief are part of the human experience in our fallen world. Even Jesus experienced grief. In Isaiah 53:3, the prophet referred to the Messiah as "despised and rejected by men, a man of sorrows and acquainted with grief" (ESV).

When my husband died, I experienced a depth of grief I had never known. Still, the Bible tells us we do not grieve as those who have no hope.[7] Loss, however deep, reminds us that this world is not all there is. Life here is temporary. The pain of loss vividly communicates to us that this world is merely a train station, not our final destination.

While these reminders can help us experience joy in practical ways, the process is not always easy. Nor is it doable in our own strength. We don't muster up true joy by plastering a smile on our faces and pretending life is perfect because we follow Christ. Remember, we have a choice. We can strive to *chase* joy *against* our circumstances. Or we can *receive* joy *regardless of* our circumstances because of whom we belong to. Which will you choose? And what will you do with the joy you receive?

## Share the Harvest

When we think of sharing joy with others, the apostle Paul's exhortation to "rejoice with those who rejoice" often comes to mind (Romans 12:15). The question is, how?

My friend Carrie creates the most beautiful greeting cards. Her cards are works of art for every occasion. Greeting card companies talk about sending the very best. For me, the very best is one of Carrie's creations because they bring me joy. Another friend, Jennifer, is a self-confessed chocoholic. Giving her chocolate, regardless of her circumstances, always makes her day better. Still another friend loves to receive flowers. The sight and scent of floral bouquets on her table bring her joy.

Are these pleasures what the Bible talks about when it refers to sharing joy? Cards, chocolates, and flowers are nice. They are also temporary. Sharing the biblical fruit of joy, however, yields eternal impact. So what does sharing biblical joy look like?

## Rejoice in Sharing the Good News

I will always remember the first time someone surrendered their life to Christ when I shared the gospel. Our mutual joy exceeded anything I could have imagined. New birth occurred right before my eyes. And it was my privilege to play a small part as I witnessed a life transformed.

Joy comes from understanding our purpose, and Paul reminded the Corinthian church our purpose is to be ministers of reconciliation.[8] What joy there is in knowing someone will live in the presence of God for eternity because we understood our purpose!

## Rejoice in Teaching God's Word

You might be thinking, *Wait a minute, I'm not a teacher. This one doesn't apply to me.* We forget teaching is not limited to a vocational career or an educational degree. Teaching can be as simple as communicating something to someone who doesn't know what you know.

King David understood the connection between the joy of a restored relationship with God and teaching others about His Word. David wrote Psalm 51 against a backdrop of sin, guilt, and conviction. Guilt wracked him for committing adultery with Bathsheba and then having her husband, Uriah, killed. In verse 12, David pleaded with God, "Restore to me the joy of Your salvation." His request did not end there. He added in verse 13, "Then I will teach wrongdoers Your ways." David knew that with restored joy came the responsibility to teach others what he had learned.

The apostle John also understood this: "What we have seen and heard we proclaim to you also, so that you too may have fellowship with us; and indeed our fellowship is with the Father, and with His Son Jesus Christ. These things we write, so that our joy may be made complete" (1 John 1:3–4). Teaching others brought fulfilling joy.

## Rejoice in Encouraging the Weary

I had always thought of the apostle Paul as a strong, persevering man. Nothing got him down, and nothing stopped him from sharing the gospel. Weary? Not Paul. Discouraged? Not this man.

Then I was reminded of passages such as 2 Corinthians 7:5, where Paul wrote, "When we came into Macedonia our flesh had no rest, but we were afflicted on every side: conflicts on the outside, fears inside."

Or in 2 Corinthians 11:24–28, where he detailed his suffering:

> Five times I received from the Jews thirty-nine lashes. Three times I was beaten with rods, once I was stoned, three times I was shipwrecked, a night and a day I have spent adrift at sea. I have been on frequent journeys, in dangers from rivers, dangers from robbers, dangers from my countrymen, dangers from the Gentiles, dangers in the city, dangers in the wilderness, dangers at sea, dangers among false brothers; I have been in labor and hardship, through many sleepless nights, in hunger and thirst, often without food, in cold and exposure. Apart from such external things, there is the daily pressure on me of concern for all the churches.

Despite all these trials, Paul also wrote about his pride in the Corinthian believers and how their encouragement and concern for him filled him with overflowing joy.[9]

### *Rejoice in Influencing Lives for Eternity*

Remember Venn diagrams from high school math—overlapping circles that share a common field? Those describe how our spheres of influence interconnect. Everyone has at least one such overlap. The overlapping spheres in my own life include family, church friends, Bible study class, writing colleagues, readers, and clients. The people in one sphere may not know any of the people in the other spheres. Yet I have the opportunity to influence each of these groups because they all know me.

How many different groups is God allowing *you* the opportunity to influence?

English preacher Charles Spurgeon understood the connection between joy and influence when he wrote, "This blessed grace of joy is very contagious. . . . Holy joy will oil the wheels of your life's machinery.

Holy joy will strengthen you for your daily labour. Holy joy will beautify you, and . . . give you an influence over the lives of others."[10]

The apostle Paul also made the same connection. He used his influence with the Philippian believers to urge them to live in unity, reminding them this would complete his joy.[11] And two chapters later, he exhorted them to stand firm in their faith, while calling them his "joy and crown" (Philippians 4:1).

## Rejoice in Others' Growth

Have you ever experienced a mentoring relationship? If you haven't, I pray you do someday soon. I have been mentored, and I have also mentored others. One thing both relationships have in common is joy in growth. Whether regarding my own growth or the growth of the one I'm mentoring, joy is the big red bow that wraps up the relationship.

I can relate to Paul when he told the church in Rome, "The report of your obedience has reached everyone; therefore I am rejoicing over you" (Romans 16:19). Or when he told the Thessalonians, "You are our glory and joy" (1 Thessalonians 2:20). John experienced a similar association when he wrote, "I have no greater joy than this, to hear of my children walking in the truth" (3 John v. 4).

## Rejoice in the Evidence of God's Existence

As I wrote this chapter, I found myself wondering: Of the nine displays of the fruit of the Spirit, why is the loss of joy one that Christians seem to especially mourn? Why does our joy appear to be the repeated target of Satan's efforts?

Could it be that the very existence of joy—a gladness not dependent on our circumstances but instead flowing from the Lord Himself—is actually evidence of God's existence? Let's close our exploration of the Spirit's fruit of joy with a passage from Acts 14:8–17. Paul and Barnabas were on their first missionary journey, testifying to the good news of salvation through Jesus Christ. After Paul healed a man born lame, the crowds attempted to worship him and Barnabas as gods. Of course Paul stopped them and pointed them back to the living God, the creator of the universe. Then Paul added, "In the past, [God] let all nations go their own way. Yet he has not left himself without testimony: He has shown kindness by giving you rain from heaven and crops in their seasons; he provides you with plenty of food and fills your hearts with joy" (vv. 16–17 NIV).

"He provides you with plenty of food *and* fills your hearts with joy." Might it be that a testimony to God's existence is not just His physical provisions but also His provision of joy? No wonder the enemy works intently to spoil our joy!

We can kindle joy by sharing greeting cards, chocolate, flowers, and other gifts. Still, the resulting gladness is a temporary shadow of what the Holy Spirit offers. In sharing joy, go for the gold, and don't settle for anything less than sharing the fruit of eternal joy!

## APPLICATION QUESTIONS

1. How has your suffering or the suffering of a loved one caused you to give up on joy?
2. Joy comes when we recognize how God is working out His purposes in us even through suffering. Think about a season of suffering you have experienced. How did God grow your relationship with Him through that time?
3. Describe a time when you were able to comfort or encourage someone else because of the comfort God gave you in a similar situation.
4. How has discontent decreased your joy?
5. How has busyness for God diminished the joy of relationship with Him?
6. In what ways has your relationship with God become a duty—an obligation?

7. In what area of life are you in the *have-to* stage? What needs to change for you to move to *want-to* or, finally, to *get-to*?
8. When was the last time you shared the gospel with someone? What prevents you from sharing the gospel more often?
9. How is God calling you to increase someone else's joy through encouragement this week?
10. How can you help in the spiritual growth of others by volunteering in your church? Ask your pastor(s) where the needs are. (Be sure there's a soft chair behind them in case they fall—pastors aren't always used to people offering to help!)

CHAPTER 4

# The Soul of Our Fruit Is Peace

I paced alone in a small hotel room three thousand miles from home in a foreign country. Waves of panic wracked my body. Rapid, shallow breaths fed the panic, and the panic fed the shallow breaths—a vicious circle holding me captive in its center. Although I was a long-term Christian and an accomplished executive for a financial services firm, I harbored a secret known only to my husband: panic attacks. Peace? A concept as foreign as the country I was in.

You may never have suffered panic or anxiety attacks. Still, most of us have experienced some level of fear or anxiousness, perhaps instigated by an alarming situation clearly out of our control. A terminal prognosis, loss of a loved one, a broken relationship, a prodigal adult child, even something as simple as nightmares . . . the circumstances can be as varied as our lives.

## Recognize the Enemy's Tactics

One of Satan's frequent temptations prompts us to view our situation as too big. Too big for us and too big for God. That we're at the mercy of our circumstances, and our circumstances have no mercy. We believe the lie that the only reasonable option is to give up and give in to fear. The devil accomplishes this by targeting three significant areas in life: peace with God, relational peace, and situational peace.

## *Peace with God*

A relationship with God the Father through faith in the sacrifice of Christ the Son brings peace through the indwelling Holy Spirit. We know that. The devil knows it too. And our enemy works overtime to cause us to doubt our salvation. Just as we saw with the fruit of joy, doubts about our relationship with God can also disturb our peace.

Another tactic the devil uses is to cause us to focus on our lack of worthiness. God chose us and saved us by His grace—an unmerited, undeserved gift. Still, we might think we need to prove to God He made the right choice. That even though we were not worthy *before* salvation, we can work at being worthy to *keep* our salvation. The possibility of losing what we didn't deserve to begin with can lead to many sleepless nights.

Yet another way the devil works to interfere with our peace is to cause us to define God by the attributes of earthly fathers. However, even the best of them are flawed. It's easy to carry our view of our earthly father over to our heavenly Father. Was or is your father abusive? Insensitive? Cold and uncaring? Untrustworthy? Absent? The enemy pounces with more of his lies. *God is no different. And the hard things you are experiencing is proof. If God were a loving Father, He would not allow you to suffer this way. And even if He does care, maybe He just doesn't see you.*

Satan works to sow seeds of doubt in God's character, ways, timing, and Word. Despite the reality that the devil cannot undo our salvation, we're prevented from resting in the assurance of our restored relationship with God.

## *Relational Peace*

Do you have any difficult people in your life? Arrogant people who exude superiority based on physical or social differences? People who sow division and strife because they must be right all the time? Selfish people whose only priority is to always come out on top? Yup. I have a few of those folks in my life too. Then again, I probably have a few people in my life who harbor negative feelings about me. And the division rarely remains contained. Instead, it seeps into every area of connection until the relationship crumbles.

Not only do we passively go along with the devil's efforts to destroy relationships, but at times we take an active part. Try having a political conversation with someone who disagrees with you. Families have been torn apart during the past several presidential elections because of political differences. Parents have even withheld their children from grandparents' visits. And yes, this happens more often than you might suppose.

When the enemy encourages us to build walls instead of bridges with other people, agitation replaces peace in our relationships.

### *Situational Peace*

Satan also uses circumstances to attack our peace in powerful ways. For several years after my husband died, I developed a bad habit of living in the future. I would tell myself, "When this happens, life will be better. When that happens, life will be better." I had fallen for the lie that peace was dependent solely on my situation.

We worry about past events, present activities, and future happenings. In his book *The Thing Beneath the Thing,* Steve Carter notes, "Whenever we focus on yesterday or tomorrow, we're missing out on the present moment. This is one of the great tricks of the enemy to pull us from this moment into the events that took place at another time or into the worry of what tomorrow will bring."[1]

These worries are all tied to our desire for control, whether of our own lives or the lives of those we love. Control is what we want most and have the least. The devil dangles it in front of us, always just out of reach. And control is tied to pride, which is not a surprise since pride caused Satan's fall from heaven.[2]

Why is this important enough to us to sacrifice the fruit of peace? Perhaps because control announces to the world that I am important. It proclaims to all that my agenda reigns supreme. And control ensures my convenience is prioritized.

To obstruct our peace, Satan employs methods targeting this need for control. Martyred missionary Jim Elliot observed, "The devil has made it his business to monopolize on three elements: noise, hurry, crowds. . . . He will not allow quietness."[3]

*Noise.* I don't handle *quiet* well. When I'm alone, my first instinct is to turn on sound: an old movie, a playlist, the radio, or a podcast on my laptop while I work. Not loud, just running in the background—but still noise. Jim Elliot's observation hit me squarely in the heart. And I know I'm not alone in this. What is it about quiet that makes us uncomfortable? I have attended meetings where a silent pause of a mere five seconds will cause people to nervously jump into the discussion just to break the quiet, although they had no intention of speaking.

*Hurry.* The smoothest, most peaceful day can be upended in an instant. All it takes is a glance at my watch and the realization that I should have left ten minutes earlier for a medical appointment. My heart rate increases, I grab my car keys, and I'm racing out the door. You can probably conclude the rest of the story. I fidget at every red light, scramble to find a parking space (of course the parking lot is full), and finally enter the building only to press the elevator call button four times as I wait. Is it any wonder that when the nurse takes my usually normal blood pressure, it's now elevated? Hurrying pulls us away from any sense of peace, replacing it with distress and a fear of failing to meet someone else's expectations.

*Crowds.* Crowds can be affirming—until they're not. When I'm at a concert with like-minded people who share my enjoyment of the performers, our mutual pleasure adds to my delight. But if I'm surrounded by angry people or those who don't share my values, I might feel pressured into going along with the majority despite my misgivings. Large groups of people make it easier to go with the flow, abandoning our sense of right and wrong. Satan wants us to fear standing against the majority. He tempts us to hide in the anonymity a crowd provides, hoping we'll forget that nothing is hidden from God's sight.[4]

It's time we think about peace not from the perspective the devil wants us to have but from God's perspective and His best for us!

## Nurture a Right Perspective

Why do we fall for the devil's lies? Perhaps it's because he plays to our deepest doubts and fears.

### *Our Ways*

We think maybe the devil is right. My circumstances are disastrous and God is not stepping in. Maybe the situation is too big for Him. Or perhaps He's too busy to bother with my issues. And like the apostle Peter, who focused on the waves instead of on Jesus, we allow the wind and waves of our storm to convince us we're on our own. After all, God's peace must be missing if we struggle with troubles in life.

### *God's Ways*

God wants us to know we're missing His peace because we're defining it all wrong!

A story has been told to illustrate our frequent confusion surrounding the definition of peace:

> A king offered a prize to the artist in his kingdom who painted the best picture of peace. Many artists tried. The king examined all the beautiful pictures and was especially drawn to two. Now he had to select a winner between them.
>
> The first picture was of a calm lake. The lake mirrored the peaceful towering mountains all around it. Overhead, fluffy white clouds dotted a blue sky. All who saw this picture described it as a perfect picture of peace.
>
> The other picture also included mountains. But that's where the similarity ended. These were rugged and bare. Rain fell from an angry sky as lightning flashed across the mountains. A foaming waterfall tumbled down the side of a cliff. This picture did not appear peaceful at all. However, when the king took a closer look, he noticed a tiny bush growing through a crack in a rock behind the waterfall. And in the bush, a mother bird had built her nest. There, surrounded by a rush of angry water, the bird sat on her nest in perfect peace.

> Which picture do you think won the prize? The king chose the second picture.
>
> "Because," explained the king, "peace does not mean to be in a place where there is no noise, trouble, or hard work. Peace means to be in the midst of all those things and still be calm in your heart. That is the real meaning of peace."[5]

God never promised us a life free of trouble in our broken world. When speaking of His coming death, Jesus told His disciples, "These things I have spoken to you so that in Me you may have peace. In the world you have tribulation, but take courage; I have overcome the world" (John 16:33). Peace *despite* trouble. All too often we equate peace with the *absence* of trouble. However, the only way to experience peace in a broken world is to start with the most important relationship of all—the relationship Satan wants us to forget or, at the very least, minimize.

## *Who Do You Belong To?*

How would you describe who you belong to? The easy answer for a Christian is "*God*." The more difficult question is, Who is God? How do you describe Him, and how do His titles and attributes relate to the fruit of peace God intends for His children to possess? Think about it a moment, and let's explore the answers.

The devil wants us to believe God is not big enough to meet our needs. We fall for this lie again and again. *God isn't big enough.* Of course, we would never actually say those words. Good Christians don't say things like that.

Yet this was the message I communicated in the past through my worry, fear, and anger when life failed to follow my agenda. Then I made excuses for my behavior. Maybe you've uttered similar rationalizations. "I can't help my emotions. It's how God made me."

I threw myself into prayer, Bible study, and ministry. But relying on external activities, even spiritual ones, was another futile attempt to control life in my own strength.

Once I ruled out physical causes requiring a medical solution, I realized what I really needed was to elevate my perspective of God.

### *How Big Is Your God?*

In his book *The Knowledge of the Holy*, A. W. Tozer wrote, "What comes into our minds when we think about God is the most important thing about us."[6] Everything in our Christian life—including the fruit of the Spirit—flows from our understanding of who God is. The devil is well aware of this, sometimes more than we are. So I began a journey of exploring God's names and attributes as He revealed Himself in His Word. Psalm 9:10 tells us those who know God's name are able to trust Him, and I wanted to trust Him more than I had in the past. In the process, I realized I had severely limited my view of God.

If you find yourself living the Christian life in your own strength, trying harder but not experiencing the peace God promised, consider—really consider—who God says He is. For example, Genesis 1:1 begins by introducing God as Elohim, the mighty creator God. He created the universe and everything in it, including planets and stars. And from childhood, the way we think about those stars influences our perspective of who He is. We teach children nursery rhymes such as "Twinkle, Twinkle, Little Star," singing about how stars are like little diamonds in the sky.

"Little star" and "like a diamond"—no wonder we're not impressed when we read God made the stars and hung them in place. Lurking in the back of our minds is the image of a jeweler grasping tweezers to place a diamond in its setting. Because we've minimized stars in our thinking, the unintended consequence is that we minimize their Creator.

Time for a reality check. Thermonuclear fusion in the core of the star we call our sun releases energy throughout our solar system. The hot plasma of our sun has a diameter of more than eight hundred thousand miles and converts four million tons of matter into energy every second. And all those other twinkling little stars in our night sky? Each one is a similar fireball. There is nothing little about stars. And there is nothing little about the God who created them.

What crisis are you facing today? Even if we're not facing a crisis now, what awaits us tomorrow? Will you join me in committing to trust the one who hung the stars in space? If He can do that, He can certainly handle whatever comes our way.

Just as God wants us to define peace in light of our relationship with Him, He also wants us to define peace as a Person, not a thing.

### Peace Is a Person

The problem with wishing for more peace is that such wishes often imply peace is a commodity—something we receive in measured amounts. At times I wish this were true. Running low on peace? No problem. I'll stop by the local store and buy a pound or two to get me through my current struggle. But peace is not a product to be purchased or an item weighed and packaged in a bag or box.

Peace is a Person. More than 2,700 years ago, the prophet Isaiah wrote of the coming of the Prince of Peace.[7] Jesus Christ entered this world of sin and discord for one purpose. He came to reconcile us to the Father—to restore peace to the relationship broken by our sin. Peace *with* God always precedes the peace *of* God. The Prince of Peace paid the price to give us peace with God and with others. How costly was that price? He gave up the glories of heaven to die a torturous death on a cross for you and me. In doing so, the Prince of Peace became our source of peace.

It is no coincidence that in each of the apostle Paul's New Testament letters, he began with the greeting "grace and peace," in that order. Grace always precedes peace. God extends His gracious gift of relationship through salvation in Jesus Christ, the Prince of Peace. And peace with God always follows. The order never changes.

Paul emphasized this point in his letter to the church in Rome. He wrote, "Since we have been justified through faith, we have peace with God through our Lord Jesus Christ, through whom we have gained access by faith into this grace in which we now stand" (Romans 5:1–2 NIV). Did you notice the order? Our peace comes through Jesus Christ—peace we receive by faith as we obtain the salvation God graciously provides. Author Britt Mooney said it this way: "We can't work to get peace. We move and live *from* it."[8]

This peace is not merely a possibility, it's a promise. In John 14:27, Jesus said, "Peace I leave you, My peace I give you; not as the world gives, do I give to you. Do not let your hearts be troubled, nor fearful." Do we take Him at His word? This promise addresses both the existence of fear as well as the extent of our control over it. And that brings us to our next step: recovery and growth.

## Recover and Grow

I struggled with those occasional panic attacks for almost twenty years as I climbed the corporate ladder while also teaching Bible studies and leading small groups at church. And I felt like a spiritual failure. A hypocrite. A fraud. Both as a corporate executive and even more as a follower of Christ and a ministry leader. I had tried everything a good Christian is supposed to do, including prayer, reading the Bible, and memorizing and meditating on Scripture. And my attempts to recover peace were a failure.

Before we continue, please know that peace-stealing issues such as anxiety and depression are not always "fixed" by simply following a to-do list of behavioral steps. A chemical imbalance may require additional medical support. And talking ourselves out of anxiety or depression is rarely the answer. Still, the foundational causes can often be spiritual. So let's examine practical ways to address spiritual causes with spiritual solutions. Those solutions begin with an all-out pursuit—but not the pursuit you might expect.

### *Pursuing the Right Goal*

My goal had been to recover peace. That makes sense, right? After all, peace is what I was missing. Everything I did was for the sole purpose of recovering what was lost. Of course, all those spiritual disciplines are important. However, the foundational issue I failed to address was my definition of peace. Remember how God defines peace? It's not a thing; it's a Person. Which did I desire more: a feeling of peace, or intimacy with the Person of peace?

This brings us back to the question, Who do we belong to? Yes, through Jesus Christ we have a restored relationship with the Father.

And yes, He brings peace because He *is* peace. Yet how eagerly do we pursue intimacy with Him simply for the sake of the relationship rather than for what we can get from the relationship? Do we first seek God's heart or His hand?

King David wrote in Psalm 42:1–2:

> As the deer pants for the water brooks,
> So my soul pants for You, God.
> My soul thirsts for God, for the living God.

David did not write, "My soul pants for Your peace" or "My soul pants for Your love." No, David wrote about a soul-deep thirst for God Himself. He understood that all the benefits of relationship flow from a wholehearted pursuit of intimacy with our Creator and Redeemer.

The prophet Isaiah also noted that the benefit of peace flows from the priority of keeping our focus on the Lord rather than on obtaining peace. Isaiah wrote, "The steadfast of mind You will keep in perfect peace, because he trusts in You" (Isaiah 26:3). When we pursue God with all our hearts, souls, and minds, peace will follow. What does that look like in our lives today?

## *Cutting Through the Noise, Hurry, and Crowds*

How do we cut through the devil's use of noise, hurry, and crowds to recover the fruit of peace? We pray! I confess my issue has not been knowing I need to pray; my issue has been my timing. All too often I turn to prayer reactively rather than proactively. And while praying anytime is always good, it's even better to follow Jesus's example.

In his gospel, Luke recorded, "Jesus often withdrew to lonely places and prayed" (5:16 NIV). Jesus went to a lonely place to pray, but He wasn't alone. He was with His Father. Luke wrote this observation immediately after noting that crowds of people came to hear Jesus's teaching and experience healing. The Son answered the pressure of noise, hurry, and crowds by slipping away for time alone with His Father, encompassed by the peace that comes from God alone.

Notice the word *often*. For Jesus, prayer wasn't only reactive; it was His practice. We nurture peace when we practice speaking to God throughout each day instead of waiting for a crisis before turning to our heavenly Father.

### Mistaken Focus

Recovering our peace may also require addressing a mistaken focus. There's nothing wrong with praying for peace when a crisis occurs. However, if peace remains elusive despite a regular practice of prayer in addition to crisis prayers, it may be time for a little self-evaluation.

*Have I made this issue an idol?* If not receiving what I asked for makes me angry or bitter at God, have I raised this request to the level of an idol? Of course, I would never intentionally worship an idol. But idols are not limited to statues of wood or stone. Idols can also be good things and precious people. If an unmet desire causes me to doubt God's goodness, that desire has become an object of worship competing for the love that belongs to God.

*Do I have unreasonable expectations in a broken world?* We don't have to look far to realize our world is sin-sick. This brokenness touches every area—nothing and no one is exempt. So why are we shaken when things don't work out the way we want? Why do we allow our peace to be snatched away over the slightest circumstance that fails to meet our expectations? Let's not allow the brokenness around us to make us doubt God's goodness and steal our peace.

*Have I redefined who God is?* It's easy for Christians—even mature Christians—to fall into the trap of redefining God according to their own desires. We say God is worthy of our worship, then question His actions when they don't line up with our plans. We talk about suffering in the abstract, then become angry or bitter when suffering becomes personal. Yet surely if God is God, His sovereignty will bring ultimate good out of everything He does.

## Flipping the Script

Are you a worrywart? I wasn't—until I experienced a significant life change. After my husband died, for the first time in my life I was living completely on my own. A year and a half later, a pandemic struck. That's when my previously nonexistent imagination churned out a continuous flood of what-ifs. What if I became sick while living alone? Who would take care of me? What if I depleted my finances? What if a hurricane damaged my South Florida home? What if I had a need I couldn't meet on my own? What if . . . ? What if . . . ? What if . . . ?

Are you plagued by your own what-ifs? What if the diagnosis is cancer? What if the prognosis is terminal? What if my prodigal refuses to return? What if I lose my job?

What-ifs have afflicted humanity since the beginning of creation. It's what Eve believed in the garden when she fell for Satan's lies and ate the forbidden fruit. *What if God is keeping the best for Himself?*

It's what the ancient Israelites believed when they refused to enter the promised land for fear of the giants in the land. *What if God leads us to die at the hands of giants?*

God calls His children to trust Him despite our what-ifs. And if our what-ifs actually happen, will we still trust Him?

But what if we flipped the script on the what-ifs? What if we asked a whole new set of questions? Questions such as . . .

> *What if I take God at His word that He'll never leave or forsake me?*
> *What if I decide to stretch and exercise my faith muscles?*
> *What if I view this as an opportunity to glorify God in new ways?*
> *What if I look for occasions to be a blessing instead of focusing on being blessed?*

The apostle Peter reminds us to give our worries and anxieties to God because He cares for us.[9] If we're honest, we don't always feel as if this is true. We're caught up in the enemy's lie that our peace is dependent on our circumstances and that God doesn't see or doesn't care.

Does God truly care? Asking that question means we've forgotten the cross. The cross is proof God does care—enough to send His Son to die for us. What greater evidence could we ask for?

### *The Practice of Peace*

There's a surface peace, and then there's a peace that transcends all understanding. Paul seemed to understand the difference when he wrote to the Philippian church (Philippians 4:6–9) with instructions for conquering anxiety and receiving God's peace:

> Do not be anxious about anything, but in everything by prayer and pleading with thanksgiving let your requests be made known to God. And the peace of God, which surpasses all comprehension, will guard your hearts and minds in Christ Jesus.
>
> Finally, brothers and sisters, whatever is true, whatever is honorable, whatever is right, whatever is pure, whatever is lovely, whatever is commendable, if there is any excellence and if anything worthy of praise, think about these things. As for the things you have learned and received and heard and seen in me, practice these things, and the God of peace will be with you.

Anxiety begins with a toehold in our thought life and can quickly grow into a foothold and then a stronghold, gutting any sense of peace God wants us to have. In this passage, Paul gave steps for controlling anxious thoughts.

First, ask God for help in releasing anxious thoughts as we gratefully acknowledge His grace and mercy. When we do, God provides a level of peace beyond our understanding that guards our hearts and minds.

Then, to prevent anxious thoughts from returning, we're to fill our thoughts with things that are honorable, pure, lovely, and worthy of praise.

Finally, we need to do this not just once but practice it until it becomes a habit. When we do, *Yahweh Shalom*, the God Who Is Peace, blesses us with a strong sense of His presence.

True peace may seem impossible to attain in our broken world, but it is the Holy Spirit's gift to us through His presence in our lives. And this gift of peace is meant to be shared.

## Share the Harvest

"Thank you for telling me to calm down. I feel more peaceful now"—said no one ever!

Advising others to be more peaceful is rarely successful. And peace is not a commodity we can box up and hand to another person. So how can we share the harvest of peace? By making peace a priority in relationship.

God is personal and relational. We see this in the Trinity: Father, Son, and Holy Spirit. In addition to the fellowship within the Trinity, God created humanity for fellowship with Him. Still, our fellowship with God is built on having peace with Him: "Having been justified by faith, we have peace with God through our Lord Jesus Christ" (Romans 5:1).

Even while we were enemies of God, He gave His Son for us.[10] We probably won't ever be asked to sacrifice our children for our enemies (aren't you glad for that?). However, God does ask us to extend mercy to others, to look beyond our own hurts to be His hands and feet and heart in a world that needs to know Him. The more we grow in our own relationship with God, the more we'll value the priority He places on peace in nurturing our human relationships.

### *Peacekeeper or Peacemaker?*

When describing our relationships, we often speak of sharing love or bringing joy. However, when it comes to peace, we use unique terms. We describe people as *peacekeepers* or *peacemakers*.

Peacekeepers avoid conflict at all costs. They live by the motto "Don't rock the boat." However, the goal of peacemakers is reconciliation. They recognize healthy conflict may be necessary for reconciliation to occur.

Which one was Jesus? We have clues from His earthly ministry. He understood that real peace does not ignore conflict. True peace addresses the cause of the problem to remove it permanently. To grant us peace with God, Jesus dealt with the problem of our sin with finality, enduring the most violent personal cost possible. The goal of His earthly life and His sacrificial death centered on making peace between God and humanity.[11]

Still, some of the things He said did not sound peaceful at all. In Luke 12:51–52, Jesus told His disciples, "Do you think I came to bring peace on earth? No, I tell you, but division. From now on there will be five in one family divided against each other, three against two and two against three" (NIV).

These words might seem strange coming from the one whom the prophet Isaiah called the Prince of Peace. Jesus was a peacemaker, not a peacekeeper. And He calls us to share the fruit of peace by following His example.

The choice to believe in Christ or not has divided families through the centuries. Being a disciple of Jesus Christ means we are to say what people need to hear rather than what they may want to hear. Of course, we are to do so gently and lovingly. Avoiding conflict may be easier, but the Prince of Peace doesn't call us to take the easy way. He calls us to be peacemakers. How do we do this?

*Be an ambassador.* In his letter to the Corinthian church, the apostle Paul reminds us that we are ambassadors of Christ with a ministry of reconciliation.[12] God works through followers of Christ to spread the message of salvation: a message of reconciliation extended to sinful humanity from our holy Creator.

To have an effective message, we are called to say hard things. Most people don't enjoy coming face-to-face with their sin. But unless they do, they will never understand their need for the Savior.

I can tend toward being a people pleaser. I will happily tell people how much God loves them. But helping them see their need because of their sin? That doesn't come as easily. Still, how can people recognize the magnificence of God's holy love and mercy unless they realize how undeserving we all are to receive it?

The key is to speak the truth in love. We don't make peace by beating people over the head with a ten-pound Bible. We make peace by coming alongside and sharing our recognition of our own need. We can share the message of peace with God because we have experienced this peace for ourselves.

*Extend forgiveness.* It's one thing to extend the peace of God by telling people He has forgiven them. It's quite another when God calls us to share the fruit of peace by forgiving others when *we* have been wronged.

Since we cannot always stop people from hurting us, our creativity knows no bounds in finding subtle ways to punish them. One way is to withhold forgiveness. When we do, we end up sentencing ourselves to a life without peace.

We know God has forgiven us. We know God tells us to forgive others. Still, we may tell ourselves a different message. *They do not deserve my forgiveness. They have not been punished enough for causing me pain. They will be let off the hook if I forgive them.*

The God of all creation forgave us at the cost of the life of His Son. And He calls us to forgive others at much less cost to ourselves. When we refuse to forgive, we become our own victims, locked in a prison of resentment while gripping the key. We destroy our own peace when we fail to nurture peace with others. Failure to forgive destroys individuals, and it destroys relationships. The only one who is happy with this is Satan.

When I was a kid, liquid medicine wasn't flavored as tastefully as it is today. Even holding my nose failed to mask the bitter taste. Years later as an adult, I tended to equate extending forgiveness with swallowing a spoonful of bitter medicine.

Until.

Until I discovered the antidote for my attitude and my objections. *I* did not deserve God's forgiveness. *I* have not been punished enough for the pain I have brought to the heart of God. His forgiveness did not excuse my sin. So how could I presume to use those same objections to rationalize withholding forgiveness from others?

More importantly, all sin is first and foremost against God Himself.

He is the one who chooses to forgive us in Christ. When you and I refuse to forgive, we place ourselves in the position of playing God. Ouch!

We have been freely forgiven, and we are to freely forgive. When we do, the fruit of peace can flourish in our life *and* provide an opportunity for peace to flourish in the other person's life as they also surrender to the Holy Spirit.

Still, it's important to note that, as with extending love, while we are called to forgive, forgiveness does not condone the other person's actions. It also does not mandate reconciliation with abusive people. Reconciliation involves a process of reestablishing trust. This requires authentic remorse by the other person in acknowledging the harm they caused. We forgive to prevent resentment and bitterness from poisoning our spirit. But forgiveness is not the same as reentering an unhealthy relationship with abusers.

*Seek fellowship in faith.* Spending time with godly people encourages me in my walk with Christ to set aside anxiety, worry, and fear. Mature Christians help me maintain my spiritual balance as they come alongside to point me to Christ and His Word. The Lord will also use wise friends to point out my spiritual blind spots. This helps me share the harvest of peace with others. However, fellowshipping with other believers is not always as easy as we would like it to be.

Romans 12:18 tells us, "If possible, so far as it depends on you, be at peace with all people." *So far as it depends on me.* Matthew 5:23–24 explains what this looks like in practice. "If you are presenting your offering at the altar, and there you remember that your brother has something against you, leave your offering there before the altar and go; first be reconciled to your brother, and then come and present your offering." Whether we obey this verse or not will identify us as peacemakers or peacekeepers.

Conflict may require stepping out of our comfort zones to deal with discord. And if there's one thing I dislike even more than conflict, it's having to address it. Applying this principle has been one of the most difficult things I've faced in one particular broken relationship. Seeking reconciliation, I offered to attend counseling with this person, facilitated by a counselor of their choosing. They declined, and my heart continues to ache over this division. I cannot force reconciliation. I can, however, continue to examine my own heart to ensure resentment does not create an obstacle to a restored relationship. I've had to accept that I am not responsible for the choices of others. Still, while I cannot compel reconciliation, I can pray for softened hearts and sensitivity to the Holy Spirit's promptings—for both of us—to prepare to embrace peace when the opportunity arises.

True fellowship among followers of Jesus is a privilege. Learning to be peacemakers is not easy, but it is critical to safeguarding this treasure in the body of Christ.

We live in a world overrun by strife and division, fear and anxiety. Recognizing the enemy's tactics and understanding God's perspective equip us to nurture peace in ourselves and share the harvest of peace with others. Sharing the fruit of peace will not always *feel* peaceful. However, the Holy Spirit equips us to live out peace in our relationships with others. We're then able to move beyond emotions to reflect in our earthly relationships the restoration we have with our heavenly Father. When we do, God receives all the glory!

## APPLICATION QUESTIONS

1. How might worries about the future be controlling your thoughts or stealing your peace?
2. What current situation have you been trying to control in an attempt to gain a favorable outcome?
3. Of the three elements—noise, hurry, and crowds—which has the enemy successfully or consistently used to disrupt your peace?
4. From the parable of the king's contest, how does the king's definition of peace relate to your life today?

5. Tozer wrote, “What comes into our minds when we think about God is the most important thing about us.”[13] If this is correct, how have your thoughts about God’s nature helped or hindered your peace?
6. Why is thinking about peace as a commodity instead of a Person a barrier to experiencing the fullness of this fruit of the Spirit?
7. Consider a specific situation that spoils your peace. How might flipping the script on your what-ifs change your perspective?
8. Are you a peacekeeper or a peacemaker? How might God be calling you to make peace rather than keep peace?
9. In which of your relationships have you avoided speaking God’s words of true peace?
10. Who is God calling you to forgive? Will you share the fruit of peace by extending forgiveness to this person today?

CHAPTER 5

# The Test of Our Fruit Is Patience

When I first surrendered my life to Christ, well-meaning Christians offered advice on a variety of subjects. One memorable warning still stands out decades later: "Never pray for patience."

Patience, translated in some Bible versions as *longsuffering*, is the display of the fruit of the Spirit in response to painful circumstances and difficult people. So it's no surprise that if we ask the Holy Spirit to cultivate patience in us, He will allow situations that require us to exercise this fruit. No wonder many hesitate to pray for patience!

## Recognize the Enemy's Tactics

If patience is nurtured in the context of difficult situations, how can we know if those circumstances spring from the devil's scheming or the refining work of the Holy Spirit? The answer may be as simple as the difference between a temptation and a test. God may allow frustrating situations to arise as opportunities to test and grow our faith muscles.

The devil, however, knows consistent impatience flows from a lack of faith. Satan's goal is never to grow us through trials but to trip us up instead. Impatience embraces doubt that God knows what is best for us or that His sovereignty—His control, authority, and timing—can be trusted. We're tempted to take matters into our own hands.

Impatience rears its ugly head in situations large and small, from serious health issues that drag on to getting stuck at a red light when we're running late.

Impatience reveals that we don't believe God is who He says He is, won't do what He said He would, or won't do it quickly enough. We may not say it, but our actions proclaim, "Hey, God, you're not handling this fast enough, so it's up to me to move events and people at a quicker pace."

I easily fall into the trap of thinking my agenda and timing outweigh my heavenly Father's agenda for me. The devil doesn't need to work hard to appeal to my pride. It's almost always there, ready to be provoked the moment I believe I know my needs better than God does. Or when I view God and others as obstacles to satisfying my desires in my timing.

### *Attacking Relationships*

Impatience damages relationships. I know this firsthand, both in giving and in receiving. A rude word spoken in haste, a harsh tone of voice, my body language—perhaps rolling my eyes at the other person . . . The result? Yet another relationship suffers.

Why is impatience a frequent temptation for us? Perhaps because our spiritual enemy knows how important relationships are to God. Think about it. The very first relationship was not between Adam and Eve. It was not even between Adam and God. The first relationship was, is, and always will be between the three persons of the Trinity—a relationship between the Father, Son, and Holy Spirit of eternal unity, love, shared authority, and deference to each other.[1]

You and I are created in the image of God and are being transformed into the likeness of Christ by the power of the Holy Spirit.[2] It shouldn't surprise us that the area of relationships is one the enemy takes satisfaction in targeting.

We are saved by grace, we grow in grace, and we are called to offer grace as we respond to others. And we need grace in those relationships because people, including ourselves, are not always easy to get along with. Remember what Jesus said in Luke 6:32–33? "If you love those who love you, what credit is that to you? For even sinners love those who love them. And if you do good to those who do good to you, what credit is that to you? For even sinners do the same." Ouch!

The devil knows the Bible, sometimes better than we do. Satan twisted Scripture by quoting Psalm 91:11–12 out of context when he tempted Jesus to throw Himself down from the top of the temple. But Matthew 4 goes on to reveal how Jesus's intimate knowledge of God's Word enabled Him to accurately quote Scripture to withstand all three of the devil's temptations. Although Satan failed in his temptations of Jesus, our spiritual enemy continues his priority of attacking relationships. And tempting us to impatience is often at the top of the list.

Disrupted relationships flow from a lack of patience. Still, most people don't start their day thinking, *Today I'll yield to the temptation of impatience in my relationships.* The enemy is too sneaky to be so obvious. Often he doesn't have to do anything. He can sit back and watch our old, fallen nature do the work for him as we let our emotions rule us.

## Models of Impatience

The lie that God won't do what He said He would, or do it as quickly as we need, is not new. I often imagine biblical characters as larger-than-life. People who set an impossibly high standard of faith. But God's Word also includes those who messed up. Impatient people who are role models of what *not* to do. And their impatience was fueled by a variety of motives.

*Fear.* First Samuel 13 describes preparation for a battle between the ancient Israelites and the Philistines. The prophet Samuel had previously instructed King Saul to wait seven days until Samuel offered sacrifices to the Lord on their behalf before engaging in battle.[3] The seventh day dawned with no sign of Samuel. The ranks of the hopelessly outnumbered Israelite army dwindled even further as the people cowered and began to scatter. Fueled by fear, impatience got the better of Saul. Instead of waiting for Samuel, Saul offered the sacrifices to plead for the Lord's favor—a priestly role he had no right to perform. His impatience eventually cost him his throne.

*Anger.* The prophet Jonah lived during a time when the northern kingdom of Israel experienced harassment by the cruel Assyrians. Against this backdrop, God called Jonah to preach a message of repentance to the Assyrian capital, Nineveh. However, Jonah had no desire to see the Assyrians escape God's righteous judgment. In his impatience for vengeance, Jonah ran in the opposite direction of God's call. God employed the services of a large sea creature to bring Jonah back, and the Ninevites ultimately repented. I wish the account of Jonah ended there. But sadly, God's grace and compassion did not change the anger that fueled Jonah's impatience for divine judgment.[4]

*Unforgiveness.* When Peter asked Jesus how often he was required to forgive an offender, Jesus told a parable about two servants. One servant, owing a huge debt to his king, pleaded for the king's patience in waiting for repayment. The king went beyond delaying repayment; he forgave the entire debt. The servant then went out, found a fellow servant who owed him a much smaller debt, and demanded repayment. His fellow servant made the same plea for patience, but the first servant ordered his debtor thrown in prison. When the king learned of this, he ordered a torturous imprisonment for the first servant. Unforgiveness fueled by greed resulted in significantly worse circumstances.[5] And speaking of greed . . .

*Greed.* In Luke 15:12–13, Jesus told a parable about an impatient son who wanted to receive his inheritance. Rather than wait for his father's natural death, the son demanded his portion of the father's estate. His greed-fueled impatience soon ended when the money ran out. Then he followed his only option and returned to his father in humility and remorse.

*Lack of trust.* Last, but not least, we have Abraham, the father of the nation of Israel. The one whom God counted as righteous because of his faith.[6] The same one through whom the Messiah was prophesied to come. Abraham had exhausted his ability to wait on God ten years after the Lord first made a covenant with him.[7] This man of great faith listened to the voice of his wife instead of the voice of the Lord.[8] Ishmael, the son of his union with his wife's servant, Hagar, ushered in both domestic discord in Abraham's own family and regional discord in the Middle East that lasts even to today.

Fear, anger, unforgiveness, greed, and a lack of trust in God: deadly motives that fueled impatience in biblical times and fuel it still today. Satan delights in tempting us to be swept along by its power—a destructive power we surrender to more times than we'd like to admit. Our defense against it begins with God's perspective on the vital fruit of patience.

## Nurture a Right Perspective

During my teen years, one of our neighbors had a favorite saying. To excuse her lack of patience, she revised the adage, "Patience is a virtue, and a virtue can't hurt you." Her version: "Patience is a virtue, but too much *can* hurt you."

Really?

### *Our Ways*

We think cultivating patience is overrated and unappealing. While most Bible translations use the word *patience* in Galatians 5:22, the New International Version translates it as *forbearance*, and the King James Version uses the word *longsuffering*. Other words related to patience include *steadfastness* and *endurance*. It's bad enough that patience sounds too much like work—those synonyms make us want to run in the opposite direction!

### *God's Ways*

God wants us to know that patience is a fruit that produces the best, and often unexpected, benefits. Benefits? I wrestled with this truth for a lengthy season in my life. What benefits could possibly come from being constrained to wait for God to act? For circumstances to change?

For people to transform their behavior? (Of course, I was never the one who needed to be transformed.)

Before we can explore God's perspective on patience, it will help to review the different types of patience described in the Bible. Let's start by exploring two Greek words we translate as "patience" in the New Testament: *hupomonē* and *makrothumia*. While these words can be used interchangeably, their context usually applies to either circumstances or people.

*Hupomonē* means to remain steadfast or to endure. The ancient Greeks used this word to describe the military action of digging in and holding ground.[9] Examples of New Testament verses incorporating a form of the word *hupomonē* include:

> Let's run with endurance the race that is set before us. (Hebrews 12:1)

> The testing of your faith produces endurance. (James 1:3)

> You have perseverance and have endured on account of My name, and have not become weary. (Revelation 2:3)

The context for each of these verses is patient endurance and perseverance in the face of difficult circumstances.

*Makrothumia* is also used to communicate patient perseverance. However, it is most often used in the context of relationships. It especially refers to longsuffering and slowness to become angry with others. New Testament verses that use a form of *makrothumia* include:

> Love is patient, love is kind, it is not jealous; love does not brag, it is not arrogant. (1 Corinthians 13:4)

> With all humility and gentleness, with patience, bearing with one another in love. (Ephesians 4:2)

> Admonish the unruly, encourage the fainthearted, help the weak, be patient with everyone. (1 Thessalonians 5:14)

Did you notice the emphasis on relationships in these verses?

Which do you think is easier to practice: *hupomonē* or *makrothumia*? For me, *makrothumia* is often more challenging. You may recall learning John Donne's classic poem in school:

> No man is an island,
> Entire of itself;
> Every man is a piece of the continent,
> A part of the main. . . .
> Any man's death diminishes me,
> Because I am involved in mankind.[10]

While I appreciate this moving poem, there are times when I relate far more readily to the person who once observed, "The Christian life would be so much easier if it weren't for all the other people!"

Getting back to fruit, would you like to guess which of the two types of patience is included in the list of nine displays of the fruit of the Spirit? If you guessed *makrothumia*—patience associated with relationships—you are correct.

Since we're on the subject of relationships, what can we learn about patience by examining God's relationship with us?

## *How God Treats Us*

Our heavenly Father sets the bar high when it comes to modeling *makrothumia* to His people. His relationship with us overflows with patience. It is perfect and kind, and brings our salvation.[11]

We see God's patience manifested for at least one hundred years while Noah built the ark.[12] More than one hundred years of watching humanity's sin multiply, yet waiting patiently until the ark was completed to accomplish the salvation of Noah and his family before executing judgment.

The apostle Peter helps us understand God's patience when he described *how* God offers the gift of salvation in 2 Peter 3:9:

> The Lord is not slow about His promise, as some count slowness, but is patient toward you, not willing for any to perish, but for all to come to repentance.

Before I began studying the fruit of the Spirit, if you had asked me why God offers us the gift of salvation, I would have talked about His love, His holiness, and the need to satisfy His justice. But as we just saw, Peter also included the patience of God as a reason for continually offering salvation to sinful people.

The apostle Paul made a similar observation when he described himself in 1 Timothy 1:16 as the worst of sinners to whom the Savior displayed "His perfect patience as an example for those who would believe in Him for eternal life."

And I love how Peter affirmed what Paul said when Peter wrote, "Regard the patience of our Lord as salvation; just as also our beloved brother Paul, according to the wisdom given him, wrote to you" (2 Peter 3:15).

As I look back on my own life, I'm thankful for God's patience. Still, if you're like me, you might be thinking it's one thing for God to model patience, but it's a whole lot more difficult for us as humans. So let's look at examples of other people in the Bible—people like you and me.

### *Benefits of Practicing Patience*

We've already seen biblical examples of people who failed to be patient with the circumstances and people in their lives. King Saul, Jonah, the Prodigal Son, and Abraham all struggled with the consequences of impatience. Now let's explore two examples of people whose patience reaped great benefits.

*Abraham.* Although Abraham was also an example of impatience, he finally learned his lesson. As the writer of the New Testament book of Hebrews noted in 6:15, "Having patiently waited, he obtained the promise." After many years and a huge misstep named Ishmael, Abraham learned to patiently wait on God and received Isaac, the son God promised.

What was the benefit of Abraham's waiting on God? The immediate benefit to Abraham and Sarah was not just the birth of a son in their old age. They also benefited from the growth of their faith. And all humanity would eventually be an even greater beneficiary as Abraham's line continued by the Lord's miraculous intervention. Through this lineage, the whole world would be blessed by the coming of the Messiah—the Savior of the world.

*Joseph.* The book of Genesis recounts Joseph's experiences as he was mistreated by his brothers, sold into slavery, unjustly accused, and then imprisoned.[13] Through it all, Joseph waited on the Lord, patiently trusting God's sovereign plan. What was Joseph's benefit in cultivating patience through years of suffering? He was elevated to second-in-command over ancient Egypt. And the greater benefit? Because of his faith, trust, and patience, millions were saved from starvation, including his own family. And his actions also preserved the line of the Messiah to come. Joseph was able to tell his brothers in Genesis 50:20, "As for you, you meant evil against me, but God meant it for good in order to bring about this present result, to keep many people alive."

The benefits of patience for Abraham and Joseph extended beyond their own lives to touch countless others. Now what about our own patience?

## Benefits of Patience Today

What are the benefits of cultivating and practicing patience in our relationships? The writer of the book of Hebrews points us to the answer in Hebrews 6:10–12 (NIV).

> God is not unjust; he will not forget your work and the love you have shown him as you have helped his people and continue to help them. We want each of you to show this same diligence to

> the very end, so that what you hope for may be fully realized. We do not want you to become lazy, but to imitate those who through faith and patience inherit what has been promised.

Even if no one else notices, God sees as we extend patience to the people He has placed in our lives. Hebrews 11:6 tells us that we cannot please God without faith and that He rewards those who seek Him in faith. And in Hebrews 6:12, we see that patience in the way we treat others finds its source in faith and is rewarded with the inheritance of God's promises.

Now that we understand both Satan's schemes against the spiritual fruit of patience and God's perspective on it, how do we recover what the enemy has attacked?

## Recover and Grow

I want the fruit of the Spirit—all nine facets, as much and as fast as possible, please. Still, there's something ironic about petitioning God to give me patience *now*. I sound like a character in the classic movie, *Willy Wonka & the Chocolate Factory*. Veruca Salt boldly demanded that her desires be met immediately as she sang her song "I Want It Now." Waiting patiently? Not Veruca—and all too frequently, not me.

Before I criticize Veruca's fictional character as selfish and impatient, I need to take a long look in the mirror. How often do I—and perhaps you—seek instant gratification?

### *Our Most Important Relationship*

I often joke that *wait* is a four-letter word in more ways than one. Patient waiting does not come easily to me. We've seen how the devil uses impatience to attack our relationships, including our most important relationship with our heavenly Father. So recovering and growing *makrothumia*—patience with other people—first requires us to cultivate patience in waiting on the Lord.

The faithful believers listed in Hebrews 11 are a great example of this. They waited their entire lives for the fulfillment of God's promised salvation through the coming of the Messiah. However, verse 39 tells us they "did not receive what was promised" because it did not happen in their lifetimes.

Did you know God includes several promises in His Word specifically for those who wait on Him? The prophet Isaiah recorded a few of those promises. Isaiah 49:23 assures us, "Those who hopefully wait for [God] will not be put to shame." Other translations of this verse substitute *hope* or *trust* in the Lord instead of *wait*. The original Hebrew word communicates a hopeful waiting as we expectantly bind ourselves to God. Isaiah 64:4 reminds us, "Nor has the eye seen a God besides You, who acts in behalf of one who waits for Him." What a wonderful promise: When we wait for God, He acts on our behalf!

A third promise found in Isaiah also talks about waiting, this time in the context of running and walking. Isaiah 40:31 tells us:

> Yet those who wait for the LORD
> Will gain new strength;
> They will mount up with wings like eagles,
> They will run and not get tired,
> They will walk and not become weary.

Are you as surprised as I was to discover the key to recovering the fruit of patience is found in combining waiting *on* God and walking *with* God?

### Walking Out Our Waiting

I used to think waiting on God meant doing nothing until He acted. But the more I studied the relationship between waiting and walking with God, the more I realized waiting is active, not passive. Consider these passages that mention walking with God:

- Enoch walked with God (Genesis 5:22, 24).
- Noah walked with God (Genesis 6:9).
- God told Abram to walk before Him (Genesis 17:1).
- In Micah 6:8, the prophet recorded God's requirement for our relationship with Him:

> What does the LORD require of you
> But to do justice, to love kindness,
> And to walk humbly with your God?

In the Bible, walking refers to lifestyle. It's a picture of how we live day to day. When we walk with someone, we're moving in the same direction and at the same pace. We don't run ahead, and we don't lag behind. Walking together involves unity and fellowship. Perhaps that's why many verses in the Old and New Testaments speak of walking with God.

So how does walking with God relate to cultivating patience? Impatience compels us to follow our own direction. And impatience propels us to run ahead of God. The apostle Paul urged the church in Ephesus to "walk in a manner worthy of the calling with which you have been called . . . with patience" (Ephesians 4:1–2). Again we see the relationship between walking with God and patiently waiting on Him. We can't do either one without faith: believing God is who He says He is and that He always acts according to His perfect nature and timing.

Author and speaker Cindy K. Sproles captured our struggle in learning to wait on God during a time of her husband's recovery from critical surgery:

> I've learned, yet again, to wait! Wait on the Lord. Wait on His ways. That's our issue, us humans. We throw ourselves to our knees in a heartbeat, begging for God to help and then we try to do things on our own because our impatience gets the best of us.
>
> At this moment, I'm learning to wait.
>
> Waiting gives us a closer view of God, don't you think? I mean when we wait, we have time to look. And when we look, we see. Then it hits us . . . Oh, I get it. We're quick to say, God has this. But in our hearts, we are long to accept that as truth. Oh, how we lie to ourselves. Thank goodness, God is patient. Otherwise, we'd all be flushed away.[14]

Oh, how I wish I could not relate to Cindy's experience! But as the saying goes, "Been there. Done that. Bought the T-shirt."

Are you and I willing to wait on God while He works things out in His perfect timing? Patient waiting provides the space for God to work in a way that gives Him all the glory for the outcome as He acts on His timetable instead of ours. Waiting in this manner, we cultivate the fruit of patience in our most important relationship of all—with Him.

Even when our faith in God is solid, patience in the strongest Christian can still be eroded by natural tendencies deep within us. These can rise up and hijack our responses in a flash.

## *Motives in the Moment*

I can start my day in quiet time with the Lord, move through the day with the best of intentions to glorify Him, and then—BAM! People and circumstances pull me into instinctive responses in a blink of the proverbial eye. Let's take another look at how our motives can lead us in the wrong direction, this time from the perspective of recovering God's best for us.

*Fear and lack of trust.* I've lost count of how many times my reaction to a fearful situation is to jump into finding my own solution. I say I trust God when my actions proclaim I'm really trusting my ability to manage the situation.

Hezekiah, king of Judah, is a prime example. He was one of Judah's "good" kings. After the reign of his evil father, Hezekiah reinstated worship of the one true God and ordered the priests to repair and cleanse the temple. So far, so good, right?

Then the Assyrians showed up. They had defeated the northern kingdom of Israel, and invasion of the southern kingdom of Judah appeared to be next on their to-do list. Rather than seek God's protection, King Hezekiah listened to bad advice and entered into an alliance with Egypt—an alliance God had forbidden. In Isaiah 30:15, God spoke through the prophet to rebuke Judah and remind the people of the wiser option they did *not* choose:

> "In repentance and rest you will be saved,
> In quietness and trust is your strength."
> But you were not willing.

Such sad words: "You were not willing." How do we recover patience to wait on God when fear compels us to act on our own? God laid out the answer for Hezekiah and for us today: in repentance and rest, in quietness and trust. Stop and listen for the quiet voice of the Holy Spirit cutting through the clanging cymbals of fear echoing through our spirits. King David understood this when he wrote in Psalm 56:3–4:

> When I am afraid,
> I will put my trust in You.
> In God, whose word I praise,
> In God I have put my trust;
> I shall not be afraid.

Quietness and trust: the antidote to fear-inspired impatience. May it never be said of us that we were not willing.

*Anger fueled by unforgiveness, greed, and pride.* Anger frequently flows from a variety of sources, including unforgiveness, greed, and pride. These emotions feed off each other, almost always resulting in impatience with other people.

The things that trigger my anger are often related to a perceived violation of my rights. Someone offended me, or has what I want, or did not treat me with the respect I think I deserve. All because I've elevated my perceived rights to the position of an idol in my life. Defending my rights becomes more important than yielding to the Holy Spirit's nurture of patience.

Perhaps you can relate. For example, God calls us to forgive the offenses of others. If the other person has not *asked* for forgiveness and shows no repentance or remorse, we can become angry and impatient at their reluctance to acknowledge the offense they committed. Let's remember, however, that forgiveness is not the same as reconciliation. We are called to forgive even if reconciliation does not occur.

Impatience can also flow from anger at not having what others have. Greed, related to pride, can dictate what we think we must have regardless of whether we truly need it. Other forms of pride may be founded on an elevated view of ourselves: We're somehow more deserving than others to receive special treatment. And if we don't receive the level of treatment we think we're owed, we become impatient with those who withhold it.

These sources of impatience don't need to be especially significant. They can be as simple as another driver cutting in front of us in traffic. Our first reaction is often anger, followed by impatience with the other driver.

Of course, not all anger is sin. Righteous anger is an appropriate response to sin. It motivates us to correct injustice. But even righteous anger can become sin if we don't handle it properly, instead allowing it to settle in our spirit as bitterness or hatred. As Paul wrote in Ephesians 4:26, "Be angry, and yet do not sin; do not let the sun go down on your anger."

So what's the antidote to impatience fueled by the connection of unrighteous anger, unforgiveness, greed, and pride?

Humility.

Specifically, the humility modeled by Jesus.

Jesus gave us a beautiful illustration of this on the night He was betrayed. The Son of God—creator of the universe, the only one who had the right to be worshiped and served—knelt before His disciples and served them by washing their feet.[15]

Paul further described the humility of Jesus in Philippians 2:5–8:

> Have this attitude in yourselves which was also in Christ Jesus, who, as He already existed in the form of God, did not consider equality with God something to be grasped, but emptied Himself by taking the form of a bond-servant and being born in the likeness of men. And being found in appearance as a

> man, He humbled Himself by becoming obedient to the point of death: death on a cross.

Humility is the antidote to any concerns about relational rights. The temptation to protect and promote my rights loses its power when I reflect on what Jesus gave up for my salvation.

Still, it's not enough to recover and cultivate patience in our lives. We're also called to share this fruit with those around us.

## Share the Harvest

My natural inclination is to jump in to fix situations I see drifting in the wrong direction. But I may move too quickly in my efforts to prevent circumstances from worsening. Sometimes the best way to help others is by sharing the fruit of patience.

What does this look like?

Jesus modeled this principle with the raising of Lazarus in John 11. After Mary and Martha sent Jesus a message alerting Him to Lazarus's illness, the gospel writer records a curious order of events in verses 4 through 6:

> v. 4: "When Jesus heard this, He said, 'This sickness is not meant for death, but is for the glory of God, so that the Son of God may be glorified by it.'"
> v. 5: "(Now Jesus loved Martha and her sister, and Lazarus.)"
> v. 6: "So when He heard that he was sick, He then stayed two days longer in the place where He was."

Jesus loved this family—and He waited? He waited until Lazarus *died* before traveling to Bethany. Anyone besides me find this a strange way of showing love? Allowing Mary and Martha to experience such heart-wrenching grief when He could have prevented their pain?

Have you ever been eager to rush in to spare a loved one pain? Perhaps it was to rescue a prodigal from the consequences of a wrong choice. Or protect someone from circumstances that might cause sadness. Yet, might the Lord have been nudging you to hold back?

For many years my husband suffered from bouts of severe depression. With the onset of each episode, I tried to manage the circumstances. I worked diligently to remove any possible triggers that might set him on the path to another dark journey. But nothing I did helped. It wasn't until he came to faith in Christ that God revealed Himself to Russ as *Yahweh Rapha*, his Healer, and healed him of depression once and for all. Instead of trying to change Russ or control the circumstances, God just wanted me to share the fruit of patience with him. The result? God got all the glory!

Since patience is a facet of the Spirit's fruit that seems the most difficult for us to share, how do we begin? Sharing this fruit begins as a seed planted in the soil of God's patience with us. Without the assurance of His patience, we have none to offer others.

### *Give by First Receiving*

When I find myself short-tempered with others, one particular reminder never fails to convict me. Remember Jesus's conversation with His disciples on His last night with them? After more than three years traveling with Jesus, eating with Him, listening to His teachings, and witnessing astonishing miracles, they still failed to see Him for who He was.

Jesus comforted His followers with the news that He was going to His Father and would prepare a place for them. Instead of feeling comforted, Thomas still had questions. How could they know where Jesus was going? Thomas wasn't the only one who failed to understand. Philip followed Thomas's question with a request to "show us the Father" (John 14:8), even though Jesus had previously and publicly stated, "I and the Father are one" (10:30).

Jesus answered Philip with a question of His own. "Have I been with you for so long a time, and yet you have not come to know Me?" (14:9). I can only imagine the combination of disappointment and patience that may have tinged His voice. Those closest to Him still didn't understand, even as the clock was running out on His earthly ministry.

This isn't just about the disciples. It's about us too. How many times have you and I let Jesus down? How many times have we tested His infinite patience with us? When we ponder the unending patience Jesus extends to us, how can we not be patient with those who disappoint us? As He loves us, we are to love others. Offering patience displays that love. As Paul wrote so simply in 1 Corinthians 13:4, "Love is patient."

And it doesn't end there. When we share the fruit of patience with others, we're not only showing them love. We're also communicating hope.

### *Relationship Between Patience and Hope*

Our world is filled with people in desperate need of hope. How can extending patience help? We find a clue in 1 Thessalonians 5:14: "We urge you, brothers and sisters, admonish the unruly, encourage the fainthearted, help the weak, be patient with everyone." Look again at this list: unruly, fainthearted, weak. While Paul gave specific advice for approaching each situation, he has one answer for them all: patience.

Even though we may not be able to bring an immediate change to someone's circumstances, we can be patient with them. We've seen how unbelief, fear, or a lack of trust can contribute to an impatient attitude. When we display patience, we communicate that the situation is not hopeless. God is still in control, and we have no need to fear. Our patience with those who are struggling lets them know that although they may have given up hope, we have not.

Romans 8:25 also affirms the connection between hope and patience: "If we hope for what we do not yet have, we wait for it patiently" (NIV). And waiting patiently means doing it without grumbling.

### *Patience Is Not Noisy!*

The book of James in the New Testament is often referred to as one of the most practical letters to the early church. James addressed issues of obedience, favoritism, the untamed tongue, wisdom, and pride. In James 5:7–8, he wrote about being patient under difficult circumstances: *hupomonē*.

We all have difficult people in our lives, and the early church was no different. One problem they experienced was oppressive behavior by the wealthy, even among believers, against the poor. James urged poor and downtrodden believers to patiently wait for the Lord's return when He would set all things right.

In verse 9, James also addressed *how* they were to treat others while they waited. "Do not complain, brothers and sisters, against one another." Some translations use the word *grumble* instead of complain. An attitude of complaining is contagious. When we grumble, we not only cultivate impatience in ourselves but nurture it in others.

I confess, even when I think I'm being patient, I'm not always quiet about it. That makes the following Bible verses especially convicting for me:

> The LORD is good to those who await Him,
> To the person who seeks Him.
> It is good that he waits silently
> For the salvation of the LORD.
> (Lamentations 3:25–26)

> Rest in the LORD and wait patiently for Him;
> Do not get upset because of one who is successful in his way,
> Because of the person who carries out wicked schemes.
> (Psalm 37:7)

> My soul, wait in silence for God alone,
> For my hope is from Him.
> (Psalm 62:5)

Yet more ouches! I'm not displaying true patience in my life if I'm being noisy about it.

With one exception. We have already explored joy as a display of the fruit of the Spirit. And making a joyful noise as we patiently wait on the Lord is another way to encourage others with the fruit of patience.

Several years ago, I gave up making New Year's resolutions. This wasn't much of a sacrifice since my annual resolutions rarely made it through March. Instead, I asked the Lord for one word for each year.

One word to be a focus and influence over every area of my life for the following twelve months.

A few years ago, my word was *wait*. If I ever wondered whether I chose the word each year or God chose it for me, the question was laid to rest that year. *Wait* is not a word I would have chosen to focus on for twelve months. So I paid attention to the ways He called me to be patient. Around the half-year mark, I congratulated myself on adopting a new perspective on waiting patiently. Then I sensed the Lord nudging me again. Was I waiting with a sense of reluctance, or was I *joyfully* waiting? Did others see in me an obligatory submission to God's timing or a joyful one? And if all they saw was an obligatory response, was I truly sharing the fruit of the Spirit with them? Sigh. I knew the answer.

For the rest of that year, I purposed to wait not just patiently but also joyfully. To wait with the same glad anticipation I had while waiting for the curtain to open on a Broadway stage. To view delays and obstacles as God's welcome guidance in keeping me on *His* timetable. The result has been greater intimacy as I trust Him, and a more powerful testimony that blesses those around me.

Recognizing Satan's interest in destroying our relationships helps us guard against the temptation to impatience with those around us. And combating the devil's lies with God's perspective on patience—including our Father's patience with us—drives us to depend on the Holy Spirit for His equipping. When we lean on Him to extend patience to others, not only do they benefit, but we do too!

## APPLICATION QUESTIONS

1. How do you naturally respond to waiting?
2. Anger, fear, unforgiveness, pride: Which of these motives have tempted you to impatience? Why?

3. Why might practicing patience with people be more difficult than patience or endurance in circumstances?
4. Who in your life consistently causes you to lose patience? Why does this person trigger impatience in you?
5. Is it easier for you to be patient with acquaintances or with family members? Why?
6. How has the Lord taught you to wait on Him?
7. How might rushing to spare a loved one from pain interfere with what God is doing in that person's life? How do you know when to step in and when to wait?
8. Who in your life needs to see hope communicated through your patience with them?
9. What does it look like for your spirit to be still as you wait on the Lord?
10. Does God have you in His waiting room today? What might be preventing you from waiting joyfully?

## CHAPTER 6

# The Generosity of Our Fruit Is Kindness

The next two displays of the fruit of the Spirit are closely related. The Greek word for kindness, *chrēstotēs*, in the Galatians list of fruit is defined as moral excellence, gentleness, goodness, or kindness.[1] As you can see, it's difficult to separate this fruit from the fruit of goodness. For this chapter, we'll focus on specific aspects of kindness.

### Recognize the Enemy's Tactics

Just when you might think our spiritual enemy can't get any sneakier, he digs deep into his bag of tricks and comes up with a scheme so seemingly harmless that we easily overlook it. But it's especially injurious to nurturing the fruit of kindness. What is this subtle strategy? Omission.

As I've grown in my walk with Christ, it has become easier (I did not say easy) to recognize when I have sinned. Whether in thoughts, words, or actions, I can usually identify something I should not have done. Then I can respond to the Holy Spirit's conviction by confessing my sin and, as appropriate, making amends and reconciling with the other person.

But dealing with the omission of kindness is trickier. The other person may not realize I let an opportunity pass, and I can justify letting it go. Sin? Not really—I didn't do anything *wrong.*

Or did I? Because while sin *could* be the absence of a kindness, sin is *always* present in selfish motives.

If ever a single priority worked against cultivating kindness, it's the priority of self. Selfishness, self-interests, and self-centeredness are obstacles to kindness because kindness is, above all, other-centered. Our human nature naturally worships at the altar of the unholy trinity: me, myself, and I. Self becomes an idol. And if self had a motto, it would be "King Me!" as it marches across the checkerboard of our lives to make a grab for the throne. Sadly, we cooperate with its demand by yielding to a variety of motives that stunt the fruit of kindness.

## Common Temptations

*Pride.* When it comes to our relationship with God, the devil tempts us to believe we have earned God's favor. Therefore, God should be kind to us because we deserve it. We're better than the next guy or gal. Or at least we're not as bad as they are. Even those who understand salvation is a gracious gift of God to the undeserving may spend their lives "following the rules" to prove they are worthy of His salvation.

Applied to our relationships, an attitude of self-centeredness or pride focuses on exalting ourselves above other people. We become puffed up, wanting others to be kind to us because we deserve it more than they do. We expect others to serve us rather than offering to serve them. We view the one-another commands in the New Testament as one-way instructions, all coming to us because we are better than others. Commands such as:

- give preference to one another,
- care for one another,
- have compassion for one another,
- bear one another's burdens,
- forgive one another,
- encourage one another, and
- the sum of all of these: be kind to one another.

We need look no further than the Pharisees of Jesus's time for an ideal example of how pride, especially spiritual pride, leaves no room for extending kindness to others.

*Critical spirit.* Closely linked to pride—and motivated by it—is a critical spirit. Wrapped in a cloak of spirituality, we can withhold kindness as a way of expressing disapproval of another person's sin. Rather than risk the appearance of condoning sin, we shift to the opposite extreme. We extend a generous dose of holy self-righteousness (there's that word self again!), making it clear that when they repent and clean up their act, they will again be worthy of our kindness.

We can apply a critical spirit not only to moral issues but to differing opinions on any topic. Conversations about politics, the economy, or even the merits of hymns versus praise choruses are enough to create enemies out of friends and eliminate the slightest chance of expressing kindness.

*Scarcity mindset.* Scarcity thinking encourages the belief that we don't or won't have enough resources for our own needs, let alone the needs of others. This perspective is not limited to tangible resources. Scarcity thinking can apply to how we spend our time and attention. It can also foster an unhealthy sense of competition when we view recognition and compliments as limited commodities: If you receive a compliment, that's one less compliment available for me. We wrongly conclude that offering assistance or other types of kindness will lead to fewer opportunities for us.

Satan wants us to believe the lie that our own interests and needs are more important than anyone else's and it's up to us to "watch out for number one."

*Redefining kindness.* Satan also targets the fruit of kindness by causing us to redefine it. How? Let's explore what Jesus said in Matthew 11:28–30 about His yoke:

> Come to Me, all who are weary and burdened, and I will give you rest. Take My yoke upon you and learn from Me, for I am gentle and humble in heart, and you will find rest for your souls. For My yoke is comfortable, and My burden is light.

A yoke is a wooden bar harnessing two animals, such as oxen, to work as a team. But it's more than a farming implement—it's also a metaphor for bondage. So what do Christ's words have to do with kindness?

Some Bible translations use the words *easy* or *pleasant* ("my yoke is easy") in place of *comfortable.* Either way, it's a translation of the same Greek word: *chrēstos,* which can mean useful, easy, good, or kind.[2] Why would Jesus use a word that could be translated "kind" to describe His yoke? When I first learned the possible meanings of this word in the original Greek, I was convinced it had to be an error. And that's what our enemy wants us to do. He wants us to redefine God's Word according to our desires rather than according to what God intended.

So what did Jesus mean when He spoke of His yoke as being comfortable or easy? First, just as two animals are yoked to work as a team, a disciple of Jesus is yoked with Him, servant to Master. And when we're yoked with Jesus, the Holy Spirit equips and empowers us to discover that discipleship is a blessing, not a burden. The alternative is to be yoked to a legalistic lifestyle, attempting to earn God's approval. But a life governed by legalism produces a more difficult and painful burden, despite what the devil wants us to believe. So Jesus's yoke really is kind.

Closely related to the tactic of redefining kindness is the devil's ploy of causing us to doubt God's consistent kindness.

## *If God Isn't Kind*

Our spiritual enemy seeks to block kindness by attacking it at the source. After all, if we don't perceive God as always kind, then we can feel free to be selective in deciding if or when *we* want to be kind. How many times have we been tempted to doubt the kindness of God when we're faced with questions and observations such as:

> *If God were really kind, He'd arrange for you to have a new car instead of sinking all your cash into constant repairs.*
>
> *How can you believe God is kind when He allowed your marriage to end in divorce?*

> *If God were truly kind, He would have helped you pass your certification exam the first time instead of having to retake it. Surely a kind God would not allow your child to suffer from frequent nightmares instead of enjoying peaceful sleep.*

Once again, Satan's tactic of instilling doubt regarding God's character and ways tracks all the way back to the garden of Eden: *Did God really say . . . ?* And if He did say it, why would a kind God deny His precious children the tasty fruit of this one tree—especially considering its benefits, such as knowing good and evil?

Isn't this the same direction our thoughts can take when we think God is withholding something pleasant from us? When I start down that road, I place myself back on the throne of my life. A self-centered perspective rules; I think I know better than God how He should extend kindness to me. And that's yet another great big ouch!

As soon as we doubt even this one aspect of God's nature, our intimacy with Him is hindered. Our relationships with others are damaged. And our ability to nurture the fruit of kindness is stifled.

### *The Why Behind It All*

Satan works hard to tempt us away from cultivating kindness, even though attacking it seems like a minor goal in the grand scheme of things. But kindness is important. A single act of kindness can energize a tired spirit. Kindness can spark hope in those sunk in despair. A touch of kindness can mean the difference between giving up and going on. For all these reasons and more, the fruit of kindness is a worthy target. Satan does not underestimate the power of kindness, and neither should we.

While the devil delights in redefining both the truth and the context of kindness, we don't have to fall for his lies. What does God have to say about kindness applied to His relationship with His people?

## Nurture a Right Perspective

Early in my Christian walk, a friend introduced me to a creative spiritual exercise to help cultivate a worshipful focus. She encouraged me to make a list of words that describe God, each beginning with one letter of the alphabet from A to Z. For example, if I made a list right now, it would include: Almighty. Beautiful. Creator. Deliverer. Eternal. Faithful. Gracious. Holy. Infinite. Just. King. Wait . . . *King*?

Of course He is King. However, even as I write this chapter on kindness, the first *k* word that came to mind was *king*, not *kind*. Maybe that's because I tend to think of kindness as a human adjective. People are either kind or unkind. But God? He's, well . . . *God*. Still, we don't have any hope of being kind apart from recognizing His kindness extended to us.

### Our Ways

We think God's kindness is defined by our desires. For example, my friend Penny struggled with the knowledge of her adult son's addiction. Some might ask how a kind God could allow this to happen in a family that loves and serves Him.

### God's Ways

God wants us to know His kindness may accomplish a larger purpose than satisfying our immediate desires.

Returning to Penny's experience, the pain of her son's addiction drove Penny to her knees, causing her to intensely pursue prayer. In His kindness, God brought her son through his addiction. In the bigger picture, He also equipped Penny to write a Bible study, *Pursuing Prayer*, which God is using to equip prayer warriors in the body of Christ.

As we noted earlier, God's kindness is intertwined with His goodness. So if kindness is the tangible expression of His goodness, what does this look like from God's perspective? Was Penny's experience an exceptional display of God's kindness? As with all the facets of the fruit of the Spirit, the answers are found in how God reveals Himself in His Word.

### God's Kindness to Ancient Israel

When I want to better understand the nature and ways of God, I search the Scriptures for clues. Sometimes I need to unpack verses and interpret veiled explanations. Other times, Scripture spells out the answer for me. Jeremiah 9:23–24 (NIV) is one such passage.

The prophet Jeremiah is speaking for the Lord, communicating a message of judgment. Heartbroken, Jeremiah literally wept over Israel's idolatrous and rebellious behavior. God said that behavior would lead to a judgment of decades of exile at the hands of the cruel Babylonian Empire. That's certainly not the context in which I expected to find a statement of God's kindness. However, immediately after describing the coming judgment, God makes a clear declaration of His loving-kindness:

> "Let not the wise boast of their wisdom
> or the strong boast of their strength
> or the rich boast of their riches,
> but let the one who boasts boast about this:
> that they have the understanding to know me,
> that I am the LORD, who exercises kindness,
> justice and righteousness on earth,
> for in these I delight,"
> declares the LORD.

"I am the LORD, who exercises kindness." The Hebrew word translated as "kindness" in this passage refers to loving-kindness. Where is God's loving-kindness in Jeremiah's situation, as the nation faced exile? It's found in His promises of the nation's restoration. A few chapters later, Jeremiah recorded that their deserved judgment will be limited to seventy years[3] and the Israelites will then be restored to their land. Any doubts about God's kindness are put to rest in Jeremiah 31:3, when He described their restoration and declares, "I have loved you with an everlasting love; I have drawn you with unfailing kindness" (NIV).

Israel's exile and subsequent return isn't the only example of God's combined severity and kindness to His people. Throughout the Old Testament, God repeatedly referenced the importance of the Law and warned of the judgment faced by those who break it. In his letter to the Romans, the apostle Paul used the word *severity* to compare God's judgment to His kindness: "See then the kindness and severity of God: to those who fell, severity, but to you, God's kindness, if you continue in His kindness; for otherwise you too will be cut off" (Romans 11:22).

How can we reconcile such severity regarding the Law with God's kindness? We might begin by remembering that in order for people to recognize their need for a Savior, they must first face the reality of their own sin. Those who do not think sin is offensive to a holy God will decline salvation as needless. The severity of judgment for sin is actually a great kindness meant to awaken recognition of the need for salvation.

### *The Kindness of Salvation*

One of the first Scripture passages I memorized when I became a child of God in Christ was Ephesians 2:8–9. "For by grace you have been saved through faith; and this is not of yourselves, it is the gift of God; not a result of works, so that no one may boast." The apostle Paul provided a clear reminder that the source of our salvation is God's grace, not our own efforts.

Until I began preparing this chapter, I had not noticed the connection of those well-known verses to God's kindness. Paul opened this section of his letter by emphasizing God's grace three times in verses 5, 7, and 8. Sandwiched between these verses about grace is a proclamation of God's kindness in verse 7: "So that in the ages to come He might show the boundless riches of His grace in kindness toward us in Christ Jesus." Why has He done this? To show His grace in *kindness*.

God's kindness is repeatedly linked in the New Testament to our salvation. We find other verses such as:

> Do you think lightly of the riches of His kindness and restraint and patience, not knowing that the kindness of God leads you to repentance? (Romans 2:4)

> When the kindness of God our Savior and His love for mankind appeared, He saved us, not on the basis of deeds which

> we did in righteousness, but in accordance with His mercy. (Titus 3:4–5)

### *Kindness Exhibited by Jesus*

God's kindness in Scripture is not limited to verses specifically labeled as kind actions. As I read the Gospels, I'm moved by how frequently Jesus reached out with kindness to those in need. When Jesus healed the leper, recorded in Matthew 8:1–3, He could have healed the man with a word spoken from a distance. That's how He healed the centurion's servant in Luke 7. Instead, Jesus healed the leper with a touch. Think about how much that contact must have meant to this man who would've been considered untouchable for as long as he had been ill!

Or consider when the religious leaders brought to Jesus a woman caught in adultery: "Early in the morning He came again into the temple area, and all the people were coming to Him; and He sat down and began teaching them. Now the scribes and the Pharisees brought a woman caught in the act of adultery . . . placing her in the center of the courtyard" (John 8:2–3).

They placed her "in the center of the courtyard." Their goal was laser-focused on trapping Jesus; they cared nothing for her dignity or shame. But Jesus attended to the situation with both righteousness and kindness. First He addressed the religious leaders' sin. Then, after her accusers departed, He spoke to her with kindness and dignity as He dealt with *her* sin.

### *Seemingly Severe Kindness Today*

I have no doubt God is kind and that kindness is a fruit of the Spirit. But I'd be lying if I said I always recognize God's kindness. Can you relate? Numerous times in my life, God's kindness has not appeared kind from my perspective. Times when I've been tempted to consider the things He allows as anything but kind!

When my husband was diagnosed with pancreatic cancer and given a terminal prognosis, I did not immediately recognize God's kindness in that situation. Yet it was this severe diagnosis that caused him to receive his Savior's kind provision of salvation. Would I have chosen this painful way for Russ to come to Christ? Absolutely not. But God, who knows our hearts, knew what it would take to draw my husband into an intimate relationship with Him. God did not cause the cancer. Illness is a consequence of our broken, sin-sick world. Still, God redeemed the situation to provide Russ with the greatest kindness possible: eternal life.

My friend Barb, like Penny, is an example of someone whose heartbreaking experience might have caused many to doubt God's kindness. Barb and her pastor-husband received news no parent wants to hear when their teen son confessed his addiction to pornography. Some might ask, "How could a kind God allow this to happen to a family dedicated to His service and glory?" However, not only did God bring their son out of his addiction, but He also equipped Barb to form a ministry to parents called Hopeful Mom and to speak and write about teaching young people to navigate healthy relationships. Barb now ministers to teens and families using what she has learned. Did God cause her son to become addicted to pornography? Absolutely not. But the Lord allowed it for the ultimate good of countless families.

Because God's nature is both kind and gracious, He extends kindness to you and me, even when the situation suggests otherwise. The deceiver wants to make us doubt God's kindness. But the Holy Spirit is always at work to nurture God's kindness in our lives. With the Spirit's equipping, we have a responsibility to recover what the enemy has attacked.

## Recover and Grow

How do we recover and grow the fruit of kindness? The answer seems obvious: Just do kind things. Think kind thoughts. Speak kind words.

If it were that easy, we'd all be kinder than we are right now, and the world would be a much nicer place. But let's face it: *Kind* does not come to mind when we think about our world. And "Just do it" is not the answer. I know because I've tried that approach way too many times and failed. So what *is* the answer? The apostle Peter points us in the right direction: "Like newborn babies, long for the pure milk of the word, so that by it you may grow in respect to salvation, if you have tasted the kindness of the Lord" (1 Peter 2:2–3).

Did you notice how he linked four key items in one sentence? Scripture, growth, salvation, and kindness. We've explored how our salvation flows from God's kindness. Here, Peter noted that if we have indeed received God's kind salvation, we are to grow in our relationship with Him.

Cultivating kindness involves studying the Bible with the same eagerness an infant has for his mother's milk. Growth in all the fruit follows as we dig into God's Word, surrendering to the Holy Spirit as He helps us understand what we read. It's all possible because of the kindness of the Lord's salvation as we follow His leading.

So how do we recover and nurture kindness in practical ways? Since kindness doesn't suddenly appear without a foundation, how do we begin?

## *Step-by-Step Instructions*

In the apostle Paul's letter to the Colossian church, he described a step-by-step process for laying the foundation for nurturing kindness in our lives. Paul used the illustration of getting dressed: taking off our old self with its evil practices and clothing ourselves or putting on the new self.

> If you have been raised with Christ, keep seeking the things that are above, where Christ is, seated at the right hand of God. Set your minds on the things that are above, not on the things that are on earth. . . .
>
> Treat the parts of your earthly body as dead to sexual immorality, impurity, passion, evil desire, and greed, which amounts to idolatry. . . . In them you also once walked, when you were living in them. But now you also, rid yourselves of all of them: anger, wrath, malice, slander, and obscene speech from your mouth. Do not lie to one another, since you stripped off the old self with its evil practices, and have put

> on the new self, which is being renewed to a true knowledge according to the image of the One who created it. . . .
>
> As those who have been chosen of God, holy and beloved, put on a heart of compassion, kindness, humility, gentleness, and patience. (Colossians 3:1–2, 5, 7–10, 12)

Paul gave us a lot to chew on as we consider how to lay a foundation for kindness. He began with our motivation: new life in Christ. Apart from it, attempting to practice kindness or any other virtue is just an act of human effort. Trying harder, working smarter, and doing better, all in our own strength, are ultimately frustrating.

So Paul first established our why, then he identified attitudes and behaviors of our old nature that need to go. Paul's use of the word *rid* means "to put off,"[4] in the way we would put off the clothes we are wearing. Imagine you just completed running a summer marathon. You're hot and sweaty. You can't wait to peel off your sticky, stinky clothes and take a cool shower. This is the word picture Paul painted for us. But he didn't stop there.

The Greek philosopher Aristotle is said to have declared that nature abhors a vacuum, meaning nature will always fill empty spaces. The problem in our spiritual life is that those spaces may be filled with undesirable content. Jesus used similar imagery:

> When the unclean spirit comes out of a person, it passes through waterless places seeking rest, and does not find it. Then it says, "I will return to my house from which I came"; and when it comes, it finds it unoccupied, swept, and put in order. Then it goes and brings along with it seven other spirits more wicked than itself, and they come in and live there; and the last condition of that person becomes worse than the first. (Matthew 12:43–45)

Paul made a parallel observation when he wrote to the Philippian believers that they were to *release* their anxious thoughts, give their requests to God, and *replace* anxiety with thoughts of what is true, honorable, right, pure, lovely, and commendable.[5]

So it's no surprise that in his letter to the Colossians, after refocusing their perspective and citing what to "put off," Paul finally focused on what to "put on." Because they have already "put on the new self," previous attitudes and behaviors have no place in them. Still, it's not enough to remove the old without replacing it with something better. So Paul told them to clothe themselves with new attitudes and behaviors befitting God's chosen, holy, and beloved people. Kindness is one of the virtues he listed.

Being kind flows from our identity as God's people, empowered by the Holy Spirit as He equips us to put off the old and put on the new. The humility that comes from remembering who we belong to leads to a supernatural outflow of what God is developing in us.

## *Pride, Humility, and Kindness*

How easily pride sneaks into my attitude—and in no area more frequently than when I'm driving. It's easy to become angry at drivers who cut in front of me in a turn lane because I think they're trying to jump the line. My natural inclination is not to let them in. In those moments the Holy Spirit reminds me that pride and a critical spirit have no place in a child of God. Instead, He equips me to offer kindness even to strangers on the road.

The enemy seeks to grow pride in us as an obstacle to extending kindness. The solution is to cultivate humility, which enables us to extend kindness to others instead of waiting for them to show kindness to us. Humility offers kindness to others even when they can't repay us.

David understood this. When Saul was king of Israel, David developed a close friendship with Saul's son Jonathan despite Saul's efforts to kill David. After both Saul and Jonathan were killed in battle, David became king. Here's where the account takes an unexpected turn:

> Then the king said, "Is there no one remaining of the house of Saul to whom I could show the kindness of God?" And Ziba

> said to the king, "There is still a son of Jonathan, one who is disabled in both feet." . . . Mephibosheth, the son of Jonathan the son of Saul, came to David and fell on his face and prostrated himself. And David said, "Mephibosheth." And he said, "Here is your servant!" Then David said to him, "Do not be afraid, for I will assuredly show kindness to you for the sake of your father Jonathan, and I will restore to you all the land of your grandfather Saul; and you yourself shall eat at my table regularly." (2 Samuel 9:3, 6–7)

David had no obligation to extend kindness to Mephibosheth. After all, Mephibosheth was next in the biological line for the throne after his grandfather, Saul, and father, Jonathan. Few would have been surprised if David had followed the common practice of eliminating potential competition for his newly obtained throne. But David was not operating according to human standards. Instead, he followed the covenant he had made with Jonathan, according to Jonathan's request: "You shall never cut off your loyalty to my house, not even when the LORD cuts off every one of the enemies of David from the face of the earth" (1 Samuel 20:15).

Instead of feeling threatened by this natural heir to the throne who was in no position to repay him, David honored him with kindness. What an example for us today to set aside pride and be kind to those who can't repay us—even those who might threaten our agendas.

Maturing the fruit of kindness requires an eternal focus, an understanding of who we belong to, and a dependence on the Holy Spirit for the right motive. Only then will we be able to share kindness with a world starved for it.

## Share the Harvest

It began with a scribbled message. In the 1980s, Anne Herbert is said to have scrawled "random kindness and senseless acts of beauty" on a restaurant place mat. The rest, as they say, is history. The concept of random acts of kindness took off, and approximately ten years later, on February 17, the first National Random Acts of Kindness Day was celebrated. A foundation was even created to spread the practice.

However, being kind to others did not start with Anne Herbert. Remember what Jesus said? "Truly I say to you, to the extent that you did it for one of the least of these brothers or sisters of Mine, you did it for Me" (Matthew 25:40).

Jesus said that what we do for others is really done for Him. Have you ever considered that you and I can be kind to our Savior by being kind to others? This places kindness on a whole new level. We're not just being kind to people. Our kindnesses are an offering to the one who extended the greatest kindness of all to us.

Let's unpack how Jesus's statement can guide us in our kindness to others.

### *In Our Thoughts*

I've always considered kindness in the context of external behavior. In other words, kindness is what other people see and hear from me. But that's not where it starts.

As I tend my flower garden, I often come across volunteers. A volunteer is a plant that appears in a new place, often from seeds spread by the wind, birds, or small animals. The seed settles into the soil, watered by the rain until, hidden in the ground, it germinates and sprouts to receive the sun's rays. And all this happens without my efforts.

Much like those volunteer seedlings, kindness begins in the soil of a heart prepared by the Holy Spirit to bear fruit. As Jesus said, "The good person out of the good treasure of his heart brings forth what is good; and the evil person out of the evil treasure brings forth what is evil; for his mouth speaks from that which fills his heart" (Luke 6:45).

Here's another way to illustrate this. If you are jostled as you're carrying a full cup of water, what spills out? How about a cup filled with coffee? The point is simple: What comes out of the cup can only be what is in the cup.

For our interactions with others to be kind, our words and actions need to flow from a heart attitude that has *already determined* to be kind, regardless of who the other person is. Worthy or not. Friend or foe. And we are unable to do this apart from asking the Holy Spirit to continue His work of growing, convicting, and enabling us to produce His fruit.

## *In Our Words*

Of all the lies we teach children, one of the biggest is, "Sticks and stones may break my bones, but words will never hurt me."

Words *can* hurt, as anyone who has been on the receiving end of a verbal attack can attest. However, from a prepared heart, our words can flow with kindness to bring hope, healing, and encouragement. For example:

> There is one who speaks rashly like the thrusts of a sword,
> But the tongue of the wise brings healing.
> (Proverbs 12:18)

> Anxiety in a person's heart weighs it down,
> But a good word makes it glad.
> (Proverbs 12:25)

> Let no unwholesome word come out of your mouth, but if there is any good word for edification according to the need of the moment, say that, so that it will give grace to those who hear. (Ephesians 4:29)

Words can be used to beat down or build up. The choice is ours. The problem is, words may spill out before we can stop them. And once spoken, they can't be recaptured. My heart's cry is the same as David's, who wrote in Psalm 141:3, "Set a guard over my mouth, LORD; keep watch over the door of my lips" (NIV).

When I was a child, my mother would remind me, "Think before you speak." The word *think* has been used as an acronym to help us guard our words. Each letter reminds us of a question:

**T**—Is it True?
**H**—Is it Helpful?
**I**—Is it Inspiring?
**N**—Is it Necessary?
**K**—Is it Kind?

The adage "Engage brain before putting mouth in gear" may well apply. But even more important than engaging our brain, have we submitted to the Holy Spirit's control and conviction? Or does the sound of our voice drown out the whisper of the Holy Spirit?

### *In Our Actions*

When I first began my corporate career fresh out of college in the financial district of New York City, I became accustomed to occasionally seeing homeless people begging money for food. Well-dressed professionals passed those in need without a second glance as they proceeded into gleaming glass-and-steel skyscrapers. Family and friends cautioned me to resist the urge to give money to beggars. They worried for my safety, assumed poor choices led to the beggars' circumstances, and concluded any money received would be used for substances other than food.

Jesus told His followers to meet the needs of those around them. Feed the hungry, show hospitality, clothe the needy, and visit the sick and those in prison. He did not say anything about their deserving help. After all, if merit was the determining factor for our salvation, then He should not have saved us!

So how did I safely respond to the needy on the city sidewalks? When I had the opportunity, and as I listened to the promptings of the Holy Spirit, I offered to purchase a meal from the closest diner or fast-food restaurant. Those who were truly hungry accepted with gratitude. The others declined.

You see, kindness does not see a need, pat the person on the head, and send them off with a "Praise the Lord, God will provide." Kindness meets the needs of others in practical ways with the same tender heart God demonstrated to us.[6]

We can come up with all sorts of excuses for why a particular situation prevents us from being kind. And believe me when I say I've come up with some creative ones! But the Bible addresses every possible excuse:

> Those who are kind benefit themselves,
> but the cruel bring ruin on themselves.
> (Proverbs 11:17 NIV)

> So in everything, do to others what you would have them do to you, for this sums up the Law and the Prophets. (Matthew 7:12 NIV)

> In humility value others above yourselves, not looking to your own interests but each of you to the interests of the others. (Philippians 2:3–4 NIV)

Acts of kindness don't always require monetary expense. We can offer our time, prayers, homemade crafts, expertise, or even a shoulder to cry on. Regardless of our financial status, God has equipped each of us with the ability to express kindness in word and deed.

## *Uncomfortable Circumstances*

Before we leave this discussion, let's take a few more moments to examine the importance of kindness in relating to two opposite but equally important categories of people. Both can be uncomfortable. What does extending kindness look like in our interaction with our enemies? And what does it look like toward those who are hurting?

*Kindness to our enemies.* Acts of kindness are not always convenient. But extending kindness is not about our convenience or benefit. It is about becoming more like Christ. That's difficult enough when we're interacting with people we like, people we're neutral toward, or even total strangers. But what about people we don't like . . . or people who don't like us? What does kindness look like then?

In this situation, as in any other, sharing this fruit of the Spirit requires dependence on the Holy Spirit's equipping and leading. Kindness is, after all, His fruit. And we start with the example God set for us. The prophet Hosea described how God led His rebellious people with cords of love and kindness despite their spiritual adultery through idol worship.

Jesus said in Luke 6:35, "Love your enemies and do good, and lend, expecting nothing in return; and your reward will be great, and you will be sons of the Most High; for He Himself is kind to ungrateful and evil people." And in Matthew 5:45, Jesus reminded us that God blesses both the righteous and the unrighteous with rain.

Kindness doesn't have to involve doing something extra special. It could be simply not withholding what we would normally do. If we extend a common courtesy or kindness to others, then let's not withhold it from those who offend us. This kindness might have to begin with an intentional decision to forgive the offender.[7] (Please remember that while forgiveness is unconditional, reconciliation requires both parties to seek restoration based on biblical principles.)

*Kindness to those who are hurting.* Often when someone we know is hurting, we want to extend kindness, but we don't know how. We're afraid of saying or doing the wrong thing, so we don't say or do anything. We may even avoid that person when they need us most. We forget that sometimes the kindest thing we can do is just sit with them, offering a comforting presence.

That's what Job's three friends did (at least to begin with). The book of Job in the Old Testament recounts the great losses inflicted upon Job by Satan. Afterward, Job's friends sat with him in silence and empathy for seven days.[8] He didn't want anything else from them. Unfortunately, they then decided to share the benefit of their supposed wisdom.

We can be guilty of similar behavior. We offer unsolicited advice without knowing all the facts. Or we try to fix a problem when that's not what God has called us to do.

Kindness to hurting people can be as simple as writing a note of encouragement or letting them know we're praying for them. It can include practical help such as running an errand, helping with household chores, or offering to babysit.

After Russ died, empathy caused me to become more sensitive to the losses suffered by others. When their painful anniversaries of loss came around, I began a practice of sending a note or a card reminding them they were not alone in remembering their loved one. The first time I sent this kind of card, I wasn't sure how it would be received. Would it open old wounds of grief or be welcomed as a healing balm? The answers came quickly and repeatedly. Every recipient appreciated the kindness of being remembered—and of my remembering their loved one.

Aren't you glad God extended kindness to us even though there was—and is—nothing we could do to repay Him? Yet the Lord does expect us to respond to His kindness, not to earn His approval or score points with Him but to reflect His kindness to others. Remember Jeremiah 9:23–24 (NIV):

> "Let not the wise boast of their wisdom
>     or the strong boast of their strength
>     or the rich boast of their riches,
> but let the one who boasts boast about this:
>     that they have the understanding to know me,
> that I am the LORD, who exercises kindness,
>     justice and righteousness on earth,
>     for in these I delight,"
>         declares the LORD.

As we reflect *His* kindness, our heavenly Father delights in *our* kindness!

## APPLICATION QUESTIONS

1. How has the enemy tempted you to redefine God's kindness as you struggle with a particular situation in your life?
2. The greatest kindness we could receive is the gift of a restored relationship with God. He extends it to us through the sinless life, sacrificial and substitutionary death, and miraculous resurrection of His Son, Jesus. If you have not yet received this gift, receive it today. If you have, take time today to thank Him for His infinite kindness to you.
3. God demonstrated His kindness to us in salvation. How does He continue to express His kindness to you as you walk with Him each day?
4. Why do you think the concept of random acts of kindness is so popular?
5. What is your greatest area of struggle in expressing kindness: thoughts, words, or actions? Why?
6. How have you grown in expressing kindness compared to last month or last year?
7. Think back over this past week. How have you shown kindness to others? What opportunities to show kindness do you wish you could reclaim?
8. What do your words reveal? Are they helpful and gentle, reflecting the overflowing love you have because the Father first loved you? Or do family and friends need a microscope to detect tiny touches of kindness that occasionally leak out?
9. How do you treat those who have betrayed you or are undeserving in other ways?
10. How can you extend kindness to someone who is hurting right now?

CHAPTER 7

# The Virtue of Our Fruit Is Goodness

In our exploration of kindness, we examined the relationship between kindness and goodness. Since kindness is the outward expression of goodness, let's delve a little deeper into this foundational motive.

Everything's relative—at least that's what our culture tells us. And when it comes to virtues, if you ask five people to define *good*, you may end up with six definitions. So what is *good*?

As we explore this fruit, we'll find that perhaps, once again, we're asking the wrong question.

## Recognize the Enemy's Tactics

"Goody Two-Shoes." A hated phrase often directed at me during middle school. "Goody Two-Shoes" was always accompanied by a smirk or an eye roll. I was the teen other mothers trusted. If Ava was going to a party, then it was okay for my friends to go too. But as a young teen, the last thing I wanted was the goody-two-shoes label.

It is so typical of Satan to turn a virtue into an insult, isn't it? A character quality to be shunned instead of embraced. And this problem is not a new one.

The apostle Paul addressed the mindset of not loving anything good when he wrote to his protégé, Timothy. Paul warned Timothy about those who "will be lovers of self, lovers of money, boastful, arrogant, slanderers, disobedient to parents, ungrateful, unholy, unloving, irreconcilable, malicious gossips, without self-control, brutal, haters of good, treacherous, reckless, conceited, lovers of pleasure rather than lovers of God, holding to a form of godliness although they have denied its power" (2 Timothy 3:2–5).

Sounds a lot like our culture today, doesn't it? Human nature hasn't changed much in two thousand years. Did you notice the phrase "haters of good"? The world does not love what is good for one basic reason: Satan is the prince of this world.[1] He does not love God; therefore, he does not love anything good, because every good and perfect gift comes from our heavenly Father.[2] No wonder the devil delights in stunting the character quality of goodness in our lives. And he specializes in employing the following three major tactics.

### *Doubting God's Goodness*

We first looked at doubt as a tactic to spoil the fruit of peace and the fruit of kindness. We're back to it again here because it's such a successful strategy. Satan wouldn't keep using doubt if it wasn't so effective.

Is God always good? Adam and Eve were not convinced of God's goodness in the garden. They thought God was keeping something good from them.[3] They believed a lie and ate the fruit. However, before we complain about the trouble Adam and Eve caused for all humanity, it's time for a little honesty. How many of us would have behaved differently? Even today, we easily become distracted by our own desires, chafing under God's restrictions when He answers our prayers with a loving but firm no.

### *Wrong Self-Assessments*

Pride also has a prominent place in Satan's toolbox. We've seen it before, and it will surely show up again. While the prophet Ezekiel directed his message to the king of Tyre, many theologians believe this passage includes an indirect reference to Satan, the power behind Tyre's throne. In Ezekiel 28:2, 12–17 (NIV), we read God's words:

In the pride of your heart
  you say, "I am a god. . . ."

You were the seal of perfection,
  full of wisdom and perfect in beauty.
You were in Eden,
  the garden of God. . . .
You were anointed as a guardian cherub,
  for so I ordained you. . . .
You were blameless in your ways
  from the day you were created
  till wickedness was found in you. . . .
So I drove you in disgrace from the mount of God,
  and I expelled you, guardian cherub,
  from among the fiery stones.
Your heart became proud
  on account of your beauty,
and you corrupted your wisdom
  because of your splendor.

Pride was Satan's downfall, and he uses this same temptation to trip us up. When we think of ourselves more highly than we should, we can quickly come to believe the lie that God isn't as good to us as we deserve. Resenting God's treatment can lead us to conclude His goodness is faulty, which then leads to a root of bitterness. And bitterness will develop into a reluctance to do good to others. After all, if we're not receiving the good we think we deserve, why should we do good to anyone else?

## *Clinging to a Substitute*

Our spiritual enemy rarely comes at us through the front door. Instead, temptation often slips through a back door, an open window, any vulnerable entry point. If doubt and pride don't work, the devil will tempt us with substitutes. For example, in Romans 12:9, Paul told believers, "Detest what is evil; cling to what is good." That seems like a fairly direct command. Hate the bad, hold on to the good. So how is this twisted into temptation?

The devil can use even good things to lure us away from the Lord's plans and purposes. Financial planning, for example. That's a good thing—until . . .

Immediately after my husband died, lured by my need for security, I started focusing to an unhealthy degree on my income and savings. Was there enough to cover my living expenses? It was a good question. What was *not* good was that, not intentionally but gradually, I began to cling to something other than God's goodness. Again, there's nothing wrong with wise financial planning. The problem occurred when it became my primary source of security.

For someone else the lure might be different: a young woman clinging to her desire to be married, wondering why God hasn't sent her "the one." Parents clinging to their dream of a growing family, angry at God because of the loss of a child.

Satan has other tactics besides the three we've just covered. Here are two others in his toolbox.

*Redefining God's goodness.* Just as we can be tempted to redefine God's kindness when He doesn't meet our desires, we may want to define God's goodness by our own standards.

We see the horrors people inflict on each other and wonder, "How can a good God allow such evil to occur?" Yet if we did not have free will to choose good or evil, critics would question how a good God could keep His followers in bondage. If we are to love God, we must be free to *choose* to love, follow, and obey Him.

*Wrong motives.* It may be difficult to imagine that the devil might *want* us to do good. You might think such a tactic would backfire on him. But doing good for the wrong reasons can backfire on us instead.

I have talked to many people who are uncertain of their eternal destination. The best they can do is hope they will go to heaven. They base their hope on their long lists of good works—but how much good is good enough? They don't know. So they live in a state of uncertainty about their eternal future, always striving but never arriving.

Satan may have a powerful arsenal of temptations, but they are no match for our glorious, good God. Our first step in reclaiming the fruit of goodness begins with seeing things from His perspective.

## Nurture a Right Perspective

When I share about God's goodness with unbelievers, I often hear, "That's nice, but what's good for you is not good for me." The implication is that goodness isn't defined by one absolute standard but is relative to individual perspectives and preferences.

### *Our Ways*

We think we are the arbiters of what is good. This is not a new cultural development. Judges 21:25, written approximately 1,300 years before the birth of Jesus, tells us that "everyone did what was right in his own eyes." And Proverbs 14:12 reminds us, "There is a way that appears to be right, but in the end it leads to death" (NIV). We get into trouble when we try to define good on our own terms, often beginning with the question, "What is good?"

### *God's Ways*

God wants us to know the better question is, *Who* is good? Jesus answered this for us in Mark 10:17–18. You may recall His conversation with the rich young ruler who approached Him with a question: "Good Teacher, what shall I do so that I may inherit eternal life?" Jesus began His reply by addressing something even more important: "Why do you call Me good? No one is good except God alone."

Jesus's priority was to clarify the implication of "good." Since only God is truly good, when the young man ascribed goodness to Jesus, did he realize he was acknowledging Jesus as God? Elsewhere in the Gospels Jesus pointed to His divinity in calling Himself the Good Shepherd.[4] It was only after clarifying His identity that Jesus answered the young man's question about eternal life.

References to God's goodness abound in the Old Testament as well.

While leading the people through the wilderness from Egypt to the promised land, Moses made a bold request of God: "Please, show me Your glory!" God's answer may not have been what Moses expected. "I Myself will make all My goodness pass before you, and will proclaim the name of the Lord before you" (Exodus 33:18–19). God clearly connected His goodness to His glory.

The first fifteen verses of the prophet Nahum's short book detail God's wrath against Nineveh, capital of the cruel Assyrian Empire. Yet in the middle of this passage is verse 7: "The Lord is good." Amid verse after verse describing righteous judgment, Nahum made sure to remind his readers of God's fundamental goodness.

## *Theology Can Be Tricky, but God Is Good*

As I was writing this book, our town survived a brush with Hurricane Milton. The storm slammed into the West Coast of Florida as a category 3 hurricane. After crossing the state, it arrived in our area as a category 1. We experienced minor damage compared to other locations in Florida. After the storm passed, I heard repeated observations about God's goodness in sparing us. Those comments made me wonder: Why were we spared and others not? What about other areas that took a severe beating? Was God not "good" to them? This is where theology can get tricky.

God is good all the time. He does not change, regardless of our circumstances or the brokenness of our sin-sick world. He is good regardless of whether my circumstances don't appear as good as yours.

God is also infinite, something our finite minds struggle to grasp and explain. There are some aspects of His nature we will never fathom this side of heaven. For that, I'm glad. If we could understand everything about God, He would not be God; He would merely be an exalted human being.

This subject of God's goodness reminds me of what the prophet Habakkuk wrote:

> Even if the fig tree does not blossom,
> And there is no fruit on the vines,

> If the yield of the olive fails,
> And the fields produce no food,
> Even if the flock disappears from the fold,
> And there are no cattle in the stalls,
> Yet I will triumph in the LORD,
> I will rejoice in the God of my salvation.
> (Habakkuk 3:17–18)

Notice the prophet did not say he would rejoice that those negative circumstances occurred. He said he would rejoice "in the LORD" despite them. Circumstances are temporary and changeable. God is eternal and unchanging . . . and always good.

In whatever circumstances we find ourselves, are we willing to say:

> Even if the cancer is not healed and I can't pay my mortgage,
> Though my marriage has failed and the economy produces no jobs,
> Though the stock market tanked and pandemics abound,
> Yet I will triumph in the Lord,
> I will rejoice in the God of my salvation.

No matter what happens, God is good. Whether we understand our circumstances or not, God is good. Whether we can serve Him the way we want or not, God is good. And whether our days are difficult or easy, God is good.

Do you believe this—truly believe this in the midst of your present circumstances? Believe it in your heart and speak it aloud because it's true: God is good all the time. And all the time, God is good.

## *God's Goodness Generously Expressed*

Similar to the fruit of kindness, God often expressed His goodness in generous ways we easily recognize and appreciate. For example, when God completed the work of creation in Genesis 1:31, He "saw all that He had made, and behold, it was very good." Creation reflected the goodness of its Creator. If we think blazing sunsets in our broken world are superb works of art now, how much more exquisite must they have been before sin entered the garden of Eden?

King David acknowledged God's generous goodness when he wrote in Psalm 23:6, "Surely goodness and mercy shall follow me all the days of my life, and I shall dwell in the house of the LORD forever" (ESV). David's life was far from trouble-free, but he still rested in the assurance of God's goodness for both this life and the life to come.

The writer of Psalm 119 extolled God's Law, and noted "Your judgments are good" (v. 39) and "You are good and You do good" (v. 68). I confess, when I dwell on the various expressions of God's goodness, I don't immediately think to include His judgments and laws in that list. Yet they show us how we fall short of His holiness and help us see our need for a Savior to redeem and restore us to our heavenly Father. Does that make God's judgments and laws good? Absolutely!

In the New Testament, Jesus observed, "If you, despite being evil, know how to give good gifts to your children, how much more will your Father who is in heaven give good things to those who ask Him!" (Matthew 7:11). James wrote, "Every good thing given and every perfect gift is from above, coming down from the Father of lights, with whom there is no variation or shifting shadow" (James 1:17). And in Romans 8:28, the apostle Paul assured his readers, "We know that God causes all things to work together for good to those who love God, to those who are called according to His purpose." All things? Yes, all things. Many of us get stuck because, despite His generosity, the severity of God's goodness can also be expressed in ways that may make us uncomfortable.

### *Aligned Perspective*

Discomfort occurs when we do not align our perspective with God's perspective. We've seen how we can be tempted to question God's goodness. Of course, that's a thought most Christians keep to themselves. We quietly wonder about the cost of following God, which leads to a life ruled by fear instead of love. Still, John wrote in 1 John 4:18, "There is no fear in love, but perfect love drives out fear."

C. S. Lewis described our problem this way: "We are not necessarily doubting that God will do the best for us: we are wondering how painful the best will turn out to be."[5] We know God is good, but how well do we trust His definition of good?

Remember Psalm 119:68: God is good and He does good. That's a fact. However, as writer, speaker, and women's ministry leader Aimee Nelson explains, "God *is* good. God *does* good. But it does not always *feel* good."[6]

We get into trouble when we allow our feelings to determine whether God is good. I recently experienced a tangible application of this truth. To prepare me for a surgery, my surgeon ordered physical therapy to stretch and loosen my leg muscles. The physical therapist worked with me for my ultimate good, but the exercises and protocols he applied did not *feel* good in the moment. Okay, that's an understatement. They hurt! But the goal was to ready me for the surgery and assist my recovery.

Kindness is always good, but goodness does not always feel kind. When Jesus cleared the money changers from the temple in Matthew 21, the people He ejected would not have described Him as kind or good. And when He denounced the religious leaders as hypocrites and blind guides in Matthew 23, they saw Jesus as anything but good.

Thankfully, God's goodness is not dependent on our feelings. He gives us the good we need, not the feel-good we might want. But since we still have to deal with our emotions, how can we recover the fruit of goodness in our lives without compromising God's perspective?

## Recover and Grow

As Jesus made clear to the rich young man, no one but God is good. Yet goodness is a characteristic of the Holy Spirit's fruit in His people. Does anyone besides me feel confused by the apparent contradiction? If only God is good, does this mean we're fighting a losing battle? If we'll never be good like God, should we stop trying?

The apostle Paul provided the answer in 2 Corinthians 9:8: "God is able to make all grace overflow to you, so that, always having all sufficiency in everything, you may have an abundance for every good deed." Our ability to reflect God's goodness can only come from His provision and equipping.

So what needs to change to make this a reality in our lives?

We start by allowing God's view of goodness to influence our perspective in the following four ways.

### *Our New Perception*

*In the now-and-later.* Cultivation of the fruit of goodness is built on the confidence that we will see God's goodness now in our earthly life as well as for eternity. David echoed this in Psalm 27:13 when he wrote, "I remain confident of this: I will see the goodness of the LORD in the land of the living" (NIV). During our study of joy, we examined John 5:24. There, Jesus used the present tense when He said, "The one who hears My word, and believes Him who sent Me, has eternal life, and does not come into judgment, but has passed out of death into life." Eternal life has already begun!

*In the not-always-comfortable.* Few people enjoy being corrected, yet God also associates His goodness with correction. David wrote in Psalm 25:8, "The LORD is good and upright; therefore He instructs sinners in the way." And the writer of Hebrews noted, "He disciplines us for our good, so that we may share His holiness" (Hebrews 12:10). It has been said we are not able to receive God's *direction* if we are not willing to receive God's *correction.* Good parents provide correction, and God is a good Father.

*In the not-on-our-own.* Once again we're reminded we cannot cultivate goodness on our own. The fruit of the Spirit comes from the Holy Spirit as we surrender to Him, and that includes the fruit of goodness.

Paul wrote to the Thessalonian church, "We pray for you always, that our God will consider you worthy of your calling, and fulfill every desire for goodness and the work of faith with power" (2 Thessalonians 1:11). C. S. Lewis understood: "The Christian . . . does not think God will love us because we are good, but that God will make us good because He loves us."[7] God is the one who makes us good in Christ, enabling us to offer goodness to others.

*In the lessons learned.* Last but not least, when we focus on our circumstances, we often ask "Why?" *Why is this happening to me? Why now? Why won't God intervene?* Often it's not until we look back on difficult or painful seasons that we can see how God used those seasons for our ultimate good and His eternal glory. They might be for character building or to give us the ability to empathize with or comfort others. It may take days, weeks, years, or decades, but Romans 8:28 will always be fulfilled: "God causes all things to work together for good to those who love God, to those who are called according to His purpose."

### Our Motives

In reading the gospel accounts, have you noticed that Jesus reserved His harshest criticism not for those who lived an openly sinful lifestyle but for the religious hypocrites? Many of the religious leaders of Jesus's day were motivated by money, status, and power. They went about doing "good" for the wrong reasons. Jesus called them out[8] and warned His followers to beware those who "like to walk around in long robes, and love personal greetings in the marketplaces, and chief seats in the synagogues and places of honor at banquets . . . and for appearance's sake offer long prayers. These will receive all the more condemnation" (Luke 20:46–47).

Hypocrisy is as despised today as it was then. I know I'd much rather deal with people who are up-front about their opinions and motives, even if I disagree with them, than deal with someone who has a hidden agenda.

Since our spiritual enemy celebrates when we do good for the wrong reasons, it's important to be especially vigilant in examining our motives. For example, if our motive is to try to earn God's approval, the Bible makes it clear our salvation is by God's grace accessed through faith.[9] Or if we're doing good so others will think of us more highly, it's time to correct our motive to align with 1 Peter 2:12: We do good deeds for others to see and glorify God.

Anyone can do good for the wrong reasons, so how can we cultivate this spiritual fruit in God-honoring ways?

*Mind our approach.* Jesus warned His followers, "Be careful not to practice your righteousness in front of others to be seen by them. If you do, you will have no reward from your Father in heaven" (Matthew 6:1 NIV). Doing good for human praise negates eternal value. Eternal value is found in first connecting to the source of the fruit.

*Taste.* We begin by tasting. You might be surprised to learn how many Bible verses connect *tasting* with God's goodness or His Word. Verses such as:

> Taste and see that the LORD is good;
> blessed is the one who takes refuge in him.
> (Psalm 34:8 NIV)

> How sweet are Your words to my taste!
> Yes, sweeter than honey to my mouth!
> (Psalm 119:103)

> You have tasted that the Lord is good. (1 Peter 2:3 NIV)

Once we've tasted God's goodness for ourselves, what's next?

*Cling.* When we examined the enemy's tactics in attacking the fruit of goodness in our lives, we saw that the devil uses even good things to lure us away from the Lord's plans and purposes for us. Just as there's an idolatrous kind of clinging, there's a godly kind. It's a matter of what motivates us and whom we're trusting. Paul wrote, "Detest what is evil; cling to what is good." That's how we gain the ability to "overcome evil with good" (Romans 12:9, 21).

What does this kind of clinging look like? I once read of a widow whose husband, who had stopped to help a stranded motorist, was killed along with the motorist when a drunk driver smashed into them. A year later, when asked how she was coping, she said, "All I know is God is good. When I can't seem to do one thing in a day, when I don't understand why God would take my husband, a man with so much to give, I remind myself that God is good."[10]

Such a powerful picture of clinging to what is good! We taste and we cling. And gratitude follows.

## Our Appreciation

Satan tempts us to redefine God's goodness to fit our own desires and agendas. An effective defense begins by thanking God for His goodness as it is instead of focusing on how we want it to appear.

First Chronicles 16:34 tells us, "Give thanks to the LORD, for He is good." Theologian J. I. Packer affirmed the importance of responding to God's goodness with appreciation: "Count your blessings. Learn not to take natural benefits, endowments and pleasures for granted; learn to thank God for them all."[11] Do we limit our gratitude only to answered prayer, or are we intentional in observing and appreciating God's goodness even in ways we did not seek?

In response to a challenge by our pastor, my friend Shelia and I took time to share five things for which we were thankful. Shelia's list included seeing a doe and her fawn visit a feeder in Shelia's yard. While she had not asked God for this joyful glimpse of wildlife, she recognized it as a sweet reminder of God's goodness reflected in His creation.

Several years ago the Holy Spirit convicted me regarding the amount of time I spend asking God for things compared to the amount of time I spend thanking Him for His answers. So now, as I receive answers to prayer, I move the request to a thank-you list. Then I commit to thanking God for His goodness and mercy for at least as long as I originally prayed for the request.

## Our Equipping

Have you ever been assigned a task without the information or training to do it well? Thankfully, God doesn't do that to us. If His Word commands us to do something in one passage, we can be sure to find other passages instructing us how to do it.

Paul listed the fruit of the Spirit in his letter to the Galatians; the apostle Peter explained *how* to live a fruitful life. He wrote, "[God's] divine power has given us everything we need for a godly life through our knowledge of him who called us by his own glory and goodness" (2 Peter 1:3 NIV). Then, continuing in verse 5, he explained that we begin with faith and then make every effort to add moral excellence or goodness to our faith.

This word, *goodness*, is the same word used to describe God's attributes just two verses earlier in verse 3. Its Greek counterpart, *arete*, refers to moral excellence and virtue. The Father calls us by His own goodness. Once we respond in faith, we are then responsible for applying this standard of goodness. Our own choices and behaviors begin to reflect intimacy with our Father as we cooperate with His process of conforming us to His Son.

Remember, God is the one who gives us the power to express goodness. We don't act in our own strength. Instead, relying on His strength as we submit to the Holy Spirit, we follow His leading. Paul wrote in Ephesians 5:8–9, "You were once darkness, but now you are light in the Lord; walk as children of light (for the fruit of the light consists in all goodness, righteousness, and truth)."

Where do we find the truth Paul referred to? Start with God's Word. As we read in 2 Timothy 3:16–17, "All Scripture is inspired by God and beneficial for teaching, for rebuke, for correction, for training in righteousness; so that the man or woman of God may be fully capable, equipped for every good work." The Holy Spirit applies Scripture to our life as we surrender to His leading, and He equips us to share the fruit of goodness with others.

## Share the Harvest

Following Russ's death, I found myself rethinking my purpose. After sharing life with my husband for decades, I was suddenly a widow—a label I struggled to accept. What did "doing good" look like in this unfamiliar and unwanted stage of life?

We examined the importance of purpose when we explored the fruit of joy. We come back to it again as we examine the hands-on aspects of sharing goodness. Finding our purpose is a universal need.

Without it, life appears meaningless. Some people spend their entire life searching for purpose and never find it. Of all the books of the Bible, they most relate to Ecclesiastes, in which King Solomon lamented the futility of our earthly existence. Solomon searched for meaning in a multitude of ways, exploring pleasure, wisdom, and labor, but he came up empty every time. His conclusion finally landed him back where he should have started: A meaningful life—a life with purpose—is rooted in fearing God and keeping His commandments.[12]

Because of Jesus, Christians know they belong to the sovereign God of creation and salvation. With this assurance, we can fulfill our purpose to be His hands and feet, generously and compassionately reflecting God's goodness. We do this regardless of our circumstances . . . and at times because of them. So what are some practical ways you and I can intentionally reflect God's goodness as we "do good"?

### *Tell Others*

Sometimes, the easiest way to do good is simply to tell others about God's goodness. The psalmist wrote in Psalm 66:16, "Come and hear, all who fear God, and I will tell what He has done for my soul."

The apostle Peter practiced this when he was summoned to the home of a Roman centurion in Acts 10:38. As he shared the good news of Jesus Christ, Peter described "how God anointed Him with the Holy Spirit and with power, and how He went about doing good."

While this can be the easiest way for us to do good, it can also be the most difficult, especially when we're with unbelievers. We may become self-conscious and anxious about the possibility of being dismissed or rejected. The key is to remember it's not about us. It's about glorifying God by speaking of His goodness, not ours.

### *Spur Others On*

I recently read an account of a runner who had suffered several health challenges, including beating breast cancer. To celebrate her victory over cancer, she entered her first marathon. With each passing mile, blisters on her feet multiplied and exhaustion engulfed her. She finally sank to the ground with the finish line in sight, unable to will herself forward another step. The few remaining runners passed her until she was the only one who had not finished. But her friends knew how important this race was to her. It wasn't about winning a ribbon or a medal; it was about celebrating perseverance. So they joined her where she had stopped and surrounded her with love and encouragement. "We're so proud of you! You can do this! You already beat cancer, so we know you can do this too." They continued to cheer her on as they walked those final steps with her to the finish line.

The writer of the book of Hebrews understood the critical role of encouragement in helping us persevere. In Hebrews 10:24–25, we read, "Let's consider how to encourage one another in love and good deeds, not abandoning our own meeting together, as is the habit of some people, but encouraging one another." We need each other to help combat times of discouragement and weariness.

Later the author continued the focus on perseverance and encouragement: "Since we also have such a great cloud of witnesses surrounding us, let's rid ourselves of every obstacle and the sin which so easily entangles us, and let's run with endurance the race that is set before us" (Hebrews 12:1).

### *Do Good Sacrificially*

It's difficult enough to sacrifice for our own goals. But God calls us also to sacrificially express goodness to others. "Do not neglect doing good and sharing, for with such sacrifices God is pleased" (13:16). Let's explore several ways we may be called to put others before ourselves.

*Prioritizing the good of others over our own benefit.* The apostle Paul told believers to seek others' welfare ahead of their own.[13] That was not a natural response two thousand years ago, and it is not a natural response in our king-me culture today. Our old nature instinctively puts our own benefits first. But God desires us to be conformed to the image of His Son,[14] and Jesus set an others-first example for us to follow.

*Doing good when we're weary.* Paul also encouraged believers to "not become discouraged in doing good, for in due time we will reap, if we do not become weary. So then, while we have opportunity, let's do good to all people, and especially to those who are of the household of the faith" (Galatians 6:9–10).

Weariness is not limited to physical fatigue. Ever feel unappreciated? Taken for granted? Unnoticed? It's not easy to remain motivated to do good when our own interests are not prioritized. And it's even more difficult if we don't feel appreciated. That can be enough to cause us to give up and move on. When this happens, I find it helpful to remember who I'm serving. Yes, I'm doing good for others, but Colossians 3:23–24 reminds me that, ultimately, I'm working for the Lord. He is the one who sees and rewards.

*Doing good in humility.* The close relationship between kindness and goodness is reinforced by the necessity of humility in both.

I've always been touched by the account of the unnamed woman who anointed Jesus in Mark 14:3–6:

> While He was in Bethany at the home of Simon the Leper, He was reclining at the table, and a woman came with an alabaster vial of very expensive perfume of pure nard. She broke the vial and poured the perfume over His head. But there were some indignantly remarking to one another, "Why has this perfume been wasted? For this perfume could have been sold for over three hundred denarii, and the money given to the poor." And they were scolding her. But Jesus said, "Leave her alone! Why are you bothering her? She has done a good deed for Me."

This passage reveals two truths related to doing good with humility. First, while some English translations describe the woman's act as "beautiful," the Greek word is most often translated elsewhere in the New Testament as "good." So in anointing Jesus, this woman did a *good* thing, despite being criticized by observers.

But even more striking for me is her utter humility. Consider the circumstances. Jesus is reclining at a table with a group of men. She enters, uninvited, and interrupts their conversation by pouring expensive perfume over Jesus's head, risking severe criticism to offer her good act of worship.

*Doing good when wronged.* Jesus not only told us to love our enemies but also told us *how*: "Love your enemies, do good to those who hate you" (Luke 6:27). It's not enough to love our enemies from a distance. Jesus told us to love them in practical ways—up close and personal in ways that could be costly.[15]

This sounds a bit naive to our twenty-first-century minds, doesn't it? After all, if we follow this command, won't we be treated like doormats—someone for our enemies to walk all over? But the way evil can be overcome is not to "fight fire with fire." It's to do good in the face of evil, knowing that God is the one who will ultimately right every wrong.

Manifesting the fruit of goodness enables us to fulfill the purposes God has for us—as we read in Ephesians 2:10: "For we are His workmanship, created in Christ Jesus for good works, which God prepared beforehand so that we would walk in them."

In Matthew 5:13–16, Jesus told His followers:

> You are the salt of the earth; but if the salt has become tasteless, how can it be made salty again? It is no longer good for anything, except to be thrown out and trampled underfoot by people.
>
> You are the light of the world. A city set on a hill cannot be hidden; nor do people light a lamp and put it under a basket, but on the lampstand, and it gives light to all who are in the house. Your light must shine before people in such a way that they may see your good works, and glorify your Father who is in heaven.

Each time you and I share the fruit of goodness, we are glorifying God by how we live, and we are giving others an opportunity to glorify Him too!

## APPLICATION QUESTIONS

1. Have you been in a situation in which you were tempted to doubt or redefine God's goodness? How did you respond to that temptation?
2. When has pride tripped you up to display good works with a wrong motive? What was the result?
3. When have you found yourself clinging to something other than God's goodness?
4. When God does not answer your prayer request in the good way you think He should, how do you hold on to your faith? What is your "even if" right now?
5. When has God's goodness toward you not *felt* good? How do you respond when God's goodness comes in the form of correction or discipline?
6. Describe a time when a taste of God's generosity toward you led you to cling to His goodness.
7. How frequently do you thank God for His goodness to you in specific ways? How can you be more intentional about thanking Him regularly?
8. Who is God calling you to encourage today? How will you help them persevere?
9. Describe a time when God used a fellow believer to spur you on to persevere.
10. Think of a person who has wronged you or who considers you their enemy. How can you be generous in doing good to that person this week?

## CHAPTER 8

# The Devotion of Our Fruit Is Faithfulness

How do you determine the faithfulness of others? Do you consider whether the person is dependable or trustworthy? What if they are faithful with other people but not you? And how many times can that person mess up before you decide they are no longer faithful?

Even more important, do you and I hold ourselves to the same standard of faithfulness we hold others to?

## Recognize the Enemy's Tactics

When you think of those you would identify as faithful, who comes to mind? Besides God, who else have you seen consistently display the characteristic of faithfulness?

What if I told you Satan is a prime example of unwavering faithfulness?

Before you decide I've taken a wrong theological turn, stay with me a bit longer.

When we speak of faithfulness as a character quality, we're talking about one who is dependable, loyal, or devoted to a particular set of beliefs. We almost always view faithfulness positively. But have you considered that Satan meets this standard in a negative context?

The devil is not now, nor ever will be, equal to God by any measure. However, we often give our spiritual enemy an advantage in our lives when we underestimate him and his spiritual forces. Satan is unwaveringly faithful to his goal of undermining the Holy Spirit's work in the life of God's children. The devil cannot steal our salvation or our fruit, but he *can* manipulate temptations and circumstances as obstacles to our intimacy with our heavenly Father. And Satan is ever so faithful to this goal.

As with many of the previous displays of the fruit of the Spirit, the father of lies faithfully employs deception to make us doubt God's faithfulness. He knows that if we doubt the Lord's faithfulness to us, we'll have no reason to be faithful to Him or to others. So how can we recognize the tactic of deception?

## Silence Versus Lies

When God is silent during my troubles, I can be vulnerable to the enemy's unrelenting whispers. I know better and am improving my ability to close my ears to Satan's lies. Later in this chapter we'll explore some tools to help us do that.

Our enemy takes great delight in crashing times of divine silence with a tsunami of chatter.

> *If you're God's child, why isn't He answering your prayers?*
> *If God is really faithful, why isn't He helping you?*
> *God healed her; why isn't He healing you?*
> *If God is faithful, why did you lose your job?*

And on and on and on. Heavenly silence invaded by a cacophony of earthly noise.

We're not the first to experience this deceptive temptation, and we won't be the last. Consider the gospel account from John 11:1, 3–6 of Lazarus and his two sisters, Mary and Martha:

> Now a certain man was sick: Lazarus of Bethany, the village of Mary and her sister Martha. . . . So the sisters sent word to [Jesus], saying, "Lord, behold, he whom You love is sick." But when Jesus heard this, He said, "This sickness is not meant for

> death, but is for the glory of God, so that the Son of God may be glorified by it." (Now Jesus loved Martha and her sister, and Lazarus.) So when He heard that he was sick, He then stayed two days longer in the place where He was.

Two thousand years later, you and I have the advantage of reading *why* Jesus waited two more days: "This sickness is not meant for death, but is for the glory of God." But Mary and Martha did not know that. All they had was silence. And the enemy took full advantage of it to do his dirty work. How do we know? We see it in Mary's own words in John 11:32: "Lord, if You had been here, my brother would not have died." I can only imagine the lies whispered in her ears. *Jesus loves you? Ha! What kind of faithful love is this? You can't trust Him. When you needed Him the most He failed you!*

Oswald Chambers explained God's silence this way:

> Has God trusted you with His silence—a silence that has great meaning? God's silences are actually His answers. Just think of those days of absolute silence in the home at Bethany! . . . Can God trust you like that, or are you still asking Him for a visible answer? . . . His silence is the sign that He is bringing you into an even more wonderful understanding of Himself. Are you mourning before God because you have not had an audible response? When you cannot hear God, you will find that He has trusted you in the most intimate way possible—with absolute silence, not a silence of despair, but one of pleasure, because He saw that you could withstand an even bigger revelation.[1]

In the case of Mary and Martha, their "bigger revelation" was the return of their brother from the dead!

## *Majoring on the Minors*

A second deception is misplaced priorities. I've always found a bit of wisdom in the general advice to avoid "minoring on the majors and majoring on the minors." Or to put it another way, "Don't sweat the small stuff—because it's all small stuff." This is good advice, considering how often we stress over unimportant issues that will be forgotten years or even days later.

But our spiritual enemy is an expert at corrupting wisdom by taking it out of context, especially when it's related to the fruit of faithfulness. The devil wants us to believe we can be selective—that some things are not important enough to require faithfulness. Satan knows if we develop a habit of cutting corners in our faithfulness with the little things, we quickly become comfortable in cutting corners on *everything.*

Jesus addressed this temptation in two different parables.

In Matthew 25:14–30, He told a parable of a man going on a journey who gave three servants money to invest. Two invested wisely, but the third, who had been given the smallest amount to manage, simply returned what he had without interest. The man made a point of commending the two other servants by saying, "Well done, good and faithful servant! You have been faithful with a few things; I will put you in charge of many things. Come and share your master's happiness!" (v. 21 NIV).

Jesus also told a parable about an unrighteous manager (Luke 16:1–12), concluding with these words: "Whoever can be trusted with very little can also be trusted with much, and whoever is dishonest with very little will also be dishonest with much. So if you have not been trustworthy in handling worldly wealth, who will trust you with true riches? And if you have not been trustworthy with someone else's property, who will give you property of your own?" (NIV).

The point of both parables is cultivating faithfulness—without cutting corners in the small things. Once again, our first step is to understand our heavenly Father's perspective.

## Nurture a Right Perspective

The fruit of faithfulness comes from a foundation of faith. And faith is like a muscle: We need to exercise it to keep it healthy and strong. So before we explore our growth of faithfulness, let's take some time to identify its relationship with faith.

### *Our Ways*

We think faith is limited to religious people who worship God. We forget that everyone exercises faith to varying degrees every day. Faith always has an object. We all have faith in something. We go to sleep each evening confident that the sun will rise the next morning. Every time we reach for a light switch, we're expressing faith that electricity will provide light. When we turn on the ignition in our car, we do so in faith that the engine will start.

### *God's Ways*

God wants us to know that even the devil is motivated by faith. Satan's faithfulness in tempting Christians to stumble by taking their eyes off their Savior is powered by his faith that he can often succeed.

But for Christians, our motivation for faithfulness is rooted in faith in God. God has shown us what it means to be faithful by what He has said and how He has dealt with His people. By the power of the Holy Spirit, He gives us the gift of faith, enabling us to be faithful to Him.

### *The Unchanging Rock*

One of Jesus's most familiar parables compared wise and foolish builders. In Matthew 7:24–27, we read how the wise man built his house on the rock and it withstood the storm. But the foolish man built his house on the sand and the house fell. (If you attended Sunday school as a child, did you find yourself singing those words as you read them?)

How does this illustration of a bedrock foundation relate to God's faithfulness? God's faithfulness cannot be observed apart from His other attributes. His faithfulness upholds the way He reveals His constant love, compassion, patience, mercy, kindness, provision, goodness, forgiveness, and every other characteristic. Without faithfulness, the display of these attributes would be random, capricious, and impulsive, much like the characteristics of the false gods of the nations surrounding ancient Israel. A. W. Tozer explained, "Upon God's faithfulness rests our whole hope of future blessedness. Only as He is faithful will His covenants stand and His promises be honored."[2]

To identify God's faithfulness, let's begin with three areas: promises for His chosen people, prophecies regarding the coming of the Messiah, and promises for the church.

### *Faithful Promises for God's Chosen People*

In Genesis 12, when God called Abram out of his home country, the Lord introduced the covenant He would establish with Abram. God confirmed this covenant in Genesis 15 and then ratified it in an unusual way. During Abram's time, covenants were frequently confirmed by laying two halves of a sacrifice across from each other, leaving a path between them. The parties to the covenant would then walk between the pieces to signify that what happened to the sacrificial animal should happen to them if they broke the covenant.

But this covenant depended on God's faithfulness alone. To dramatize this, God caused Abram to fall into a deep sleep. Only then did the Lord use a "smoking oven and a flaming torch" to represent His presence passing between the pieces (Genesis 15:17).

The covenant included promises of land, descendants, and blessing upon the entire world through those descendants. This blessing of both Jews and Gentiles found its fulfillment in Jesus Christ. Although the nation waited centuries for the Messiah to arrive, God remained faithful to His promises, bringing them to fulfillment in His perfect timing.

God's faithfulness is not always expressed the way we might expect. We often think of faithfulness in terms of someone who behaves according to our desires. But God sometimes displayed His faithfulness in ways His people may not have appreciated in the moment.

For example, even after the prophet Jeremiah witnessed Jerusalem conquered and destroyed by the Babylonian Empire, he was able to proclaim God's faithfulness. In Lamentations 3:22–23, Jeremiah wrote:

> The LORD's acts of mercy indeed do not end,
> For His compassions do not fail.

> They are new every morning;
> Great is Your faithfulness.

Jeremiah proclaimed God's faithfulness as the nation was carried into exile. He knew God had not abandoned His people despite their circumstances. The prophet understood God was faithfully fulfilling His promise to discipline His nation for their sins. And the same faithfulness that exiled them would also draw them back to their promised land at the right time.

### *Faithful Prophecies of the Messiah*

Over the span of centuries, God faithfully promised the coming of His Son to restore sinful humanity to Himself. These prophecies validated Jesus's identity when He did arrive. Consider just a few of the more than three hundred fulfilled prophecies from the Old Testament that testify to God's faithfulness in even the smallest details:

> The Lord Himself will give you a sign: Behold, the virgin will conceive and give birth to a son, and she will name Him Immanuel. (Isaiah 7:14)

> As for you, Bethlehem Ephrathah,
> Too little to be among the clans of Judah,
> From you One will come forth for Me to be ruler in Israel.
> His times of coming forth are from long ago,
> From the days of eternity.
>
> (Micah 5:2)

> Rejoice greatly, Daughter Zion!
> Shout, Daughter Jerusalem!
> See, your king comes to you,
> righteous and victorious,
> lowly and riding on a donkey,
> on a colt, the foal of a donkey.
> (Zechariah 9:9 NIV)

God's faithfulness shines on the pages of the Old Testament as prophecy after prophecy is fulfilled to every last detail. And Luke 24:27 tells how Jesus Himself explained those Old Testament writings about Himself to His followers.

## Faithful Promises for the Church

My estimation of the faithfulness of others is often directly influenced by the amount of time it takes them to be true to their word. The longer I have to wait for a promise to be fulfilled, the harder it is for me to believe the other person is indeed faithful.

By that standard, God's people may have found it more and more difficult to remain convinced He would faithfully send His promised Messiah. From the first prophecy in Genesis 3:15 to the birth of Christ several thousand years later, promises were passed from generation to generation. And each succeeding generation asked the same question: When? When will Messiah finally come?

After the first advent of Jesus Christ, those questions arose again, this time about His second coming. The apostle Peter wrote that scoffers would challenge God's faithfulness: "Where is the promise of His coming? For ever since the fathers fell asleep, all things continue just as they were from the beginning of creation" (2 Peter 3:4).

Easily forgotten then—and today—is that the Lord does not change.[3] The faithful God who sent His Son to rescue us from sin's penalty is the same faithful God whose Son will return to rescue us from sin's presence for eternity.

You and I still rest in God's promises to His church, such as . . .

> In My Father's house are many rooms. . . . I am going there to prepare a place for you. And . . . I am coming again and will take you to Myself, so that where I am, there you also will be. (John 14:2–3)

> God is faithful, so He will not allow you to be tempted beyond what you are able, but with the temptation will provide the way of escape also, so that you will be able to endure it. (1 Corinthians 10:13)

> He who began a good work among you will complete it by the day of Christ Jesus. (Philippians 1:6)

We look to the time when our Savior will be faithful in promises not only of blessing but also of justice and righteous judgment. In Revelation 19, the apostle John declared,

> I saw heaven opened, and behold, a white horse, and He who sat on it is called Faithful and True, and in righteousness He judges and wages war. . . . From His mouth comes a sharp sword, so that with it He may strike down the nations, and He will rule them with a rod of iron; and He treads the wine press of the fierce wrath of God, the Almighty. (vv. 11, 15)

Jesus is not like people who make promises but fail to follow through. Because He is who He says He is, He has the power to faithfully deliver on *all* His promises.

So where does that leave you and me? How can we strengthen our faith muscles to recover and nurture a fruitful life of faithfulness today?

## Recover and Grow

Recovering and growing the fruit of faithfulness involves stretching our faith muscles. I'll be the first to admit it's easier said than done. The devil does not fight fair, and he takes full advantage of God's sovereign times of silence.

I never thought of myself as committing treason. But treason is not only an act of rebellion against a country or government. It can also involve working against the authority in my life who deserves my unreserved allegiance. That would be God. At times I have devoted myself to activities and attitudes that prioritized my comfort and convenience over His glory.

Brad Bigney, in his book *Gospel Treason*, identifies an idol as "anything or anyone that captures our hearts, minds, and affections more than God."[4] I've been guilty of this in moments of pursuing my own desires, and I'm fairly sure I'm not alone. It's so easy to be faithful to

God and the gospel when I see God working in ways I may have requested. But when He is working for my good and His glory in ways that make me uncomfortable, my faithfulness can vanish like mist in bright sunlight.

The ancient Israelites demonstrated this more than once, starting almost immediately after their miraculous deliverance from Egyptian slavery. They had witnessed—and been protected from—God's ten plagues on the Egyptians. They had walked on dry land through the miraculous parting of the Red Sea.[5] Then three days after crossing the Red Sea, they complained about a lack of water. And six weeks later they grumbled about having no meat.[6] They didn't use these exact words, but their grumbling communicated, "What have you done for us lately, God?"

Perhaps you're experiencing doubts because you've been crying out to God for a special need and He has been silent. How can we avoid a what-have-you-done-for-me-lately attitude to combat the enemy's insidious lies that God doesn't care?

## *Past Examples for Present Faithfulness*

Since our ability to nurture the fruit of faithfulness flows from God's interactions with us, how can we remind ourselves of His faithfulness in our lives? We can find clues as we explore biblical accounts of believers. Despite frequent failures, God's people recovered and cultivated their own faithfulness to Him by recalling His care for them. Illustrations of practical examples are found throughout the Bible.

*Blessings as memory prompts.* Through Moses, God warned His people to view blessings and prosperity as memory prompts:

> When you have eaten and are satisfied, you shall bless the LORD your God for the good land which He has given you.
>
> Be careful that you do not forget the LORD your God by failing to keep His commandments, His ordinances, and His statutes which I am commanding you today. (Deuteronomy 8:10–11)

*Physical reminders.* In passages such as Joshua 4 and 1 Samuel 7, God's people arranged stones as physical reminders of His faithfulness to them during specific events. In Joshua 4:1–7, the stones commemorated the nation's crossing the Jordan River. In 1 Samuel 7:12, the stone signaled the location of God's help in a decisive victory over the Philistines. Each of these displays memorialized God's faithfulness.

We can establish physical reminders today. Practices of journaling, creating artwork, or wearing a particular piece of jewelry can serve as physical reminders of the Lord's constancy.

*Celebrations.* In ancient Israel, feasts and holy days were also occasions to remind Israel of specific displays of God's faithful care. For example, we read in Exodus 12:14, 26–27:

> This day shall be a memorial to you, and you shall celebrate it as a feast to the LORD; throughout your generations you are to celebrate it. . . .
>
> When your children say to you, "What does this rite mean to you?" then you shall say, "It is a Passover sacrifice to the LORD because He passed over the houses of the sons of Israel in Egypt when He struck the Egyptians.

Today we participate in feasts and celebrations to commemorate weddings, birthdays, and anniversaries. Consider expanding this practice to include reminders of God's mercy and grace in your life and family.

As I write this, today is the sixth anniversary of my husband's Celebration of Life service. Russ's testimony included healing from depression when he received Christ as Savior—depression that had plagued him on and off for decades. At the end of the service, my pastor did something he had never done at a memorial service (and has not since): He prayed for healing for those who struggled with depression. In that moment my friend Meribeth, who had also dealt with depression for decades, was healed by God's grace. Each year since, Meribeth intentionally celebrates this memorial anniversary as a reminder of God's grace and faithfulness to her.

*Testimonies.* Consider God's faithfulness to the first-century Christians who gave their all for the spread of the gospel. Or the faith expressed by the woman who anointed Jesus with expensive perfume in Matthew 26. Jesus testified to His Father's faithfulness in preparing Him, through her action, for what would soon occur. In verses 12–13, He said of her, "When she poured this perfume on My body, she did it to prepare Me for burial. Truly I say to you, wherever this gospel is preached in the whole world, what this woman has done will also be told in memory of her."

An easy way to recall God's faithfulness is to talk about our own experience and the experiences of those who have gone before us. Personal testimonies are powerful as we share them with others. We can tell our stories and the stories of those who have influenced us. And I've noticed that the more I remind myself of how my heavenly Father has cared for me in the past, the easier it is to rest in His care for the future.

We can also learn from giants of the faith who set examples for us. Missionaries who labored in obscurity. Martyrs who trusted God's faithfulness to the end. People such as George Müller, who built orphanages to care for two thousand children in England, relying on the Lord's provision without soliciting funds; or Jim Elliot, martyred missionary, who wrote in his journal, "He is no fool who gives what he cannot keep to gain that which he cannot lose."[7]

*Communion.* Another way we can recall God's faithfulness and cultivate this fruit in ourselves is to participate in the Lord's Supper. When He took the bread, Jesus gave thanks, broke it, and gave it to His disciples, saying, "This is My body, which is being given for you; do this in remembrance of Me" (Luke 22:19). In 1 Corinthians 11:26, the apostle Paul reminded believers of Jesus's words when he wrote, "For as often as you eat this bread and drink the cup, you proclaim the Lord's death until He comes."

Think about what Paul was saying. When we participate in Communion, we proclaim the faithfulness of our heavenly Father in sending

Jesus to die for us. And we also affirm our trust in His faithfulness to return in His perfect timing.

*Songs.* Songs rehearsing God's faithfulness to His people fill the book of Psalms. King David wrote Psalm 103 as both a praise and a reminder of how faithfully God dealt with him, as we can see from the first five verses:

> Bless the LORD, my soul,
> And all that is within me, bless His holy name.
> Bless the LORD, my soul,
> And do not forget any of His benefits;
> Who pardons all your guilt,
> Who heals all your diseases;
> Who redeems your life from the pit,
> Who crowns you with favor and compassion;
> Who satisfies your years with good things,
> So that your youth is renewed like the eagle.

A number of the psalms, such as Psalm 107, rehearse the history of God's faithful dealings with the nation of Israel. And today we sing songs to recall God's faithfulness. A beloved example is "Great Is Thy Faithfulness." Inspired by Lamentations 3:22–23, Thomas Chisholm wrote the lyrics and William Runyan set them to music in 1923:

> Great is Thy faithfulness, O God my Father;
> there is no shadow of turning with Thee;
> Thou changest not, Thy compassions, they fail not;
> as Thou hast been, Thou forever wilt be.
>
> Refrain:
> Great is Thy faithfulness! Great is Thy faithfulness!
> Morning by morning new mercies I see;
> all I have needed Thy hand hath provided:
> great is Thy faithfulness, Lord, unto me![8]

The motto of the US Marines is *Semper fi,* a shortened version of the Latin phrase *semper fidelis,* "always faithful." As we recover and cultivate the fruit of faithfulness, may the Marine Corps motto apply to every child of God in Christ. And may we share the harvest of our faithfulness with every person God brings into our lives.

## Share the Harvest

I recently began to identify with a term not commonly used these days. Well, it *is* used, but not in ways I typically relate to. I'm a *steward.* And so are you.

If we think of stewards or stewardesses at all, it's often in the context of flight attendants or labor organization representatives. In this sense, stewards are those who serve others. But another meaning of stewardship is common in the Bible: A steward is someone who cares for or manages someone else's property. And faithfulness is a required characteristic of good stewards.[9]

So how does stewardship influence our ability to express and share faithfulness today?

Author Randy Alcorn describes a steward this way:

> A steward manages assets for the owner's benefit. The steward carries no sense of entitlement to the assets he manages. It's his job to find out what the owner wants done with his assets, then carry out his will.[10]

Since everything in the world belongs to God,[11] we are stewards, not owners, of what we have. As faithful stewards of what God has entrusted to us, we faithfully interact with others. And that faithfulness occurs across every area of life—our time, our talents, and more.

### *Time*

I stopped using the term "time management" a few years ago because I realized I cannot *manage* time. I can't create more time and I cannot gift myself additional time in a particular day or week, as much as I might want to. Time is not mine. I don't own it. God provides it to me for His purposes. I have access to a limited amount of time on earth, and only God knows what that amount is. We're reminded of this in Psalm 31:15: "My times are in Your hand."

We are stewards of the time allotted us on earth. We've all been entrusted with this limited gift from God. How we use it is our choice. For example, I can view the needs of others as interruptions or as opportunities to be a faithful steward. I can use the time I have to further my own interests or to minister to others.

Elisabeth Elliot, widow of martyred missionary Jim Elliot, has this to say about how we use—or don't use—our time: "'I don't have time' is probably a lie more often than not, covering 'I don't want to.' We *have* time—twenty-four hours in a day, seven days in a week."[12] She goes on to explain, "We are given the present within which to choose whom we will serve, knowing that this moment affects the next and we are accountable for it."[13]

Life is about choices. And our choices reflect our priorities. The best place to start is in prioritizing our relationship with God. This is nonnegotiable. Do you have a daily quiet time? Do you start your day with prayer? A huge shift occurred in my life when I stopped asking the Lord to bless *my* daily agenda and started asking Him for the ability to complete what *He* intended for me to do.

### *Talents*

In his first letter, Peter encouraged believers to serve as faithful stewards of the gifts God gives us for His glory:

> As each one has received a special gift, employ it in serving one another as good stewards of the multifaceted grace of God. . . . So that in all things God may be glorified through Jesus Christ, to whom belongs the glory and dominion forever and ever. Amen. (1 Peter 4:10–11)

The context of this passage mentions gifts such as hospitality, serving, speaking, and teaching. These gifts (and others listed in Romans 12:3–8 and 1 Corinthians 12:4–11), were never meant to be hoarded for our own interests alone. Rather, they are intended to benefit the body of Christ: our brothers and sisters in the Lord.

### *Possessions*

When I was discipled early in my Christian walk, a spiritual mentor advised me to hold my possessions loosely. If I held them tightly, my hands would not be free and open to receive the greater gifts God intended to give me.

Of course, God gives us material gifts to enjoy. The test comes in how we receive them and what we do with them.

I can receive God's material gifts with a resentful heart as I compare my circumstances with another's. Or I can receive His gifts with a grateful heart, knowing, as James 1:17 reminds us, that "every good thing given and every perfect gift is from above, coming down from the Father of lights, with whom there is no variation or shifting shadow."

Jesus said, "Do not store up for yourselves treasures on earth, where moth and rust destroy, and where thieves break in and steal. But store up for yourselves treasures in heaven, where neither moth nor rust destroys, and where thieves do not break in or steal; for where your treasure is, there your heart will be also" (Matthew 6:19–21). I can hoard what God has given me, or I can faithfully share my resources as the Holy Spirit prompts and enables me.

### *Spiritual Truth*

Possessions are not the only gifts God gives us. He has also given us His Word and the gospel message it contains. Of those too we are to be faithful stewards, sharing with a world that desperately needs them.

Paul likened the Christian life to a relay race. Having trained Timothy to pastor a local church, Paul urged the younger disciple to pass on the baton of the teaching he had received to others to advance the kingdom of Christ: "The things which you have heard from me in the presence of many witnesses, entrust these to faithful people who will be able to teach others also" (2 Timothy 2:2).

You and I are likewise responsible for passing on the gospel and the truths we have learned from God's Word. Psalm 145:4–7 reminds us,

> One generation will praise Your works to another,
> And will declare Your mighty acts.
> On the glorious splendor of Your majesty
> And on Your wonderful works, I will meditate.
> People will speak of the power of Your awesome acts,
> And I will tell of Your greatness.
> They will burst forth in speaking of Your abundant goodness,
> And will shout joyfully of Your righteousness.

### *Prayer*

God also calls us to be faithful in sharing the gift and privilege of prayer.

Are there particular Bible verses that seem to pierce your heart whenever you read them? First Samuel 12:23 is a challenging verse for me. The prophet Samuel had reminded the people of their repeated faithlessness, including their demand for a king like the surrounding nations had. The people responded in fear as they realized their failure to honor God as their king. But Samuel reassured them God would not reject them. Then he added, "As for me, far be it from me that I would sin against the LORD by ceasing to pray for you; but I will instruct you in the good and right way." He continued in verse 24 to encourage them to faithfully serve the Lord from that day forward.

Ouch! How many times in my life have I neglected to pray for those I believed had wronged me or, at the very least, had failed to respond the way I thought they should?

Do you and I pray for our own faithfulness *and* for the faithfulness of other Christians? For years I've used a daily prayer guide to pray for persecuted Christians. This guide encourages prayer for Christians to remain faithful to God's Word of life even in persecution and suffering. What a privilege to pray for brothers and sisters in Christ, not just for relief from persecution but also for faithfulness while being persecuted. As I continue to pray this, the Holy Spirit convicts me of how quick I am to pray for relief *from* suffering and slow to pray for faithfulness *in* suffering.

Our faithfulness to God and others cultivates hope in those whom God has placed in our sphere of influence. When we allow difficult circumstances to hijack our focus, despair and discouragement can eclipse any thoughts of hope. But when our lives reflect God's faithfulness, we communicate hope in the one who is bigger than our situation—a gift we give ourselves *and* those around us.

## APPLICATION QUESTIONS

1. How faithful are you in the small things, especially when no one is watching? Where have you been tempted to cut corners for convenience?
2. How can you guard against compromising your faithfulness in both the major issues of life and the seemingly inconsequential ones?
3. Why might some think faithfulness is secondary to other priorities? What does this devaluing of faithfulness reveal about our prioritization of trust and dependability in our culture?
4. How has God revealed His faithfulness to you in good times *and* in challenging times?
5. How can you apply the biblical examples of those who have gone before us to recover and cultivate the fruit of faithfulness in your life today?
6. How do God's fulfilled promises to the church help you remain faithful to Him today?
7. Can you identify an idol of comfort or convenience that prevents you from living faithfully? What do you need to change?
8. Who in your life has exemplified God's faithfulness?
9. How will you use reminders to cultivate faithfulness in your

life, whether blessing prompts, physical reminders, celebrations, testimonies, Communion, or songs?
10. How can you be more intentional about stewarding your time, talents, and possessions?

CHAPTER 9

# The Character of Our Fruit Is Gentleness

Have you ever played "Which one doesn't belong?" These puzzle games have been adapted for all ages, from sets of pictures for preschoolers to complicated number sequences for mathematics studies. The goal is to identify one item that does not share the same properties as others in the group. For example, a kindergartener might be asked to select the photo that does not belong in this group: apple, banana, fork, and pear.

For many Christians, gentleness appears to be the one characteristic that doesn't belong with the fruit of the Spirit. It's an admirable quality for Christians and non-Christians alike, but it may be difficult to see gentleness as a spiritual trait. And that's where we give our spiritual enemy an advantage.

## Recognize the Enemy's Tactics

Successful spiritual warfare requires an awareness not only of the devil's tactics but also of our vulnerabilities. Those weaknesses are what Satan targets. And often they're our blind spots.

Christians today play right into the devil's hands when, amid a sinful culture, we proclaim righteousness with an attitude of contempt, condemnation, and rage at those we consider evil. I imagine the devil sitting back and laughing at the damage we do to the cause of Christ. How can we expect an unbeliever to be open to the gospel after being the target of bitter denunciations? Standing up for righteousness is one thing; gloating over people's eternal destruction in hell is quite another.

So what schemes do we fall prey to that work against a gentle spirit? Five tactics are particularly effective.

### *The Thief's Methods*

*Pride.* An effective tactic against other displays of fruit, pride also works against a gentle spirit. The apostle Paul warned Christians to "not think of yourself more highly than you ought, but rather think of yourself with sober judgment" (Romans 12:3 NIV). Pride corrupts a gentle spirit on two levels: in our relationship with God and in our relationships with others.

Arrogance causes us to think we can make wise choices without submitting to the Holy Spirit's leading. We think, *I've got this. I can handle this without God's help.* This same root of pride causes alcoholics to tell their loved ones, "One drink is not a problem because I can stop when I want to."

Prideful independence from God causes us to believe we are wiser than everyone else. This attitude leads us to deal harshly with others when they don't agree with us, even bullying them to do things our way.

Pride also causes us to be judgmental. A common complaint by unbelievers about Christians is that we're better known for what we are against than what we are for. For example, the world knows Christians are pro-life and against taking unborn life. They do not see us expressing compassion for women who think abortion is their only "choice." Bottom line, our spiritual enemy celebrates when we speak the truth but not in love.

*Unconfessed sin.* Closely related to pride is the temptation to harbor unconfessed sin. Have you noticed how easy it is for us to judge and criticize the sins of others while ignoring our own? The enemy doesn't have to work hard in this department. We participate by creating hierarchies of sin, with our sin usually ranked lower in severity than the sins of others.

Jesus addressed this in the Sermon on the Mount:

> Why do you look at the speck that is in your brother's eye, but do not notice the log that is in your own eye? Or how can you say to your brother, "Let me take the speck out of your eye," and look, the log is in your own eye? You hypocrite, first take the log out of your own eye, and then you will see clearly to take the speck out of your brother's eye! (Matthew 7:3–5)

Hypocrisy, harshness, and a critical spirit often flow from unconfessed sin. As these attitudes thrive, growth of a gentle spirit can be stunted until it appears nearly nonexistent.

*Unforgiveness.* Another spiritual trap occurs when we think we're being righteous by not forgiving those who have harmed us. The devil and our culture have conditioned us to equate forgiveness with approving evil. If we forgive, we're letting the perpetrator off the hook. Shouldn't they pay for the harm they caused?

The problem is, it's almost impossible to be gentle with others if we're consumed with judging them. The apostle Paul connected forgiveness with neutralizing Satan's schemes. He exhorted the Colossian believers to forgive a repentant sinner in their midst, and he affirmed his own forgiveness of that person "so that no advantage would be taken of us by Satan, for we are not ignorant of his schemes" (2 Corinthians 2:11).

*Worry.* Just as pride is rooted in an unhealthy focus on ourselves, worry also looks inward. A certain amount of worry or fear is reasonable in unsafe situations, but fear isn't always limited to concerns about safety.

Worry and anxiety can also cause us to obsess about how to control circumstances for our comfort and convenience. Instead of surrendering to our heavenly Father's care, we focus on shortcuts to meet our needs, regardless of those around us. Maybe we push our way onto a train to grab the last remaining seat. Or we join the Black Friday crowd that tramples each other underfoot in our eagerness to be the first inside for the sales.

*Uncontrolled tongue.* I came to know Jesus as Savior when I was a young teenager. My first Bible study was a summer youth group study of the book of James. That study brought me face-to-face with the power of the tongue, a lesson I'm still learning decades later.

James did not hold back when he wrote about the power of our words in 3:5–6:

> The tongue is a small part of the body, and yet it boasts of great things.
>
> See how great a forest is set aflame by such a small fire! And the tongue is a fire, the very world of unrighteousness; the tongue is set among our body's parts as that which defiles the whole body and sets on fire the course of our life, and is set on fire by hell.

Ouch! God used James to clearly identify the source of a harsh tongue: It's set on fire by the devil's domain.

Warnings about our words are sprinkled throughout the Bible, especially in the book of Proverbs. Verses such as:

> There is one who speaks rashly like the thrusts of a sword,
> But the tongue of the wise brings healing.
>
> (12:18)

> A gentle answer turns away wrath,
> But a harsh word stirs up anger.
>
> (15:1)

A soothing tongue is a tree of life,
But perversion in it crushes the spirit.
(15:4)

Death and life are in the power of the tongue.
(18:21)

And finally back to James again in 1:26: "If anyone thinks himself to be religious, yet does not bridle his tongue but deceives his own heart, this person's religion is worthless."

Satan understands just how powerful a tool the uncontrolled tongue can be. It often reveals his four other tactics operating in us. Most concerning is that none of our enemy's tactics are forced on us. As temptations appear, we frequently incorporate them into our lives. We give a gentle spirit low priority if it's a priority at all. But God has a different perspective.

## Nurture a Right Perspective

Some people have a harsh view of God. They think the creator of the universe, the one who has held everything together through millennia, the Savior of all humanity, has more important things to be concerned about than how fragile humanity is.

### *Our Ways*

We think the God of the Old Testament is wrathful and unforgiving. We focus on Old Testament verses in which God revealed Himself as a holy, righteous judge. He is described as a consuming fire wiping out entire nations to judge sin. It's only in the New Testament that we see the gentler nature of God.

### *God's Ways*

God wants us to know He is the same God in both the Old and New Testaments of the Bible. He is holy, and He is love. He is a righteous judge, and He is merciful. He is a consuming fire, and He is gentle.

What seem to be contradictions to us are attributes that combine for a complete description of God's character and glory. Yet if you ask people to describe God's attributes, words such as *righteous, holy,* and *just* will often come to mind long before they think of *gentle.*

## *Have You Seen the Father?*

I'm glad Jesus's twelve disciples were a little dense on multiple occasions. After all, if they didn't ask the questions they did, we may not have had Jesus's answers recorded in the Gospels for us today. And we often require those explanations. For example, in John 14:1–4, Jesus told His disciples He would be leaving. But He was going to prepare a place for them, and He would return to bring them with Him. Then He said, "You know the way where I am going."

Thankfully for us, two of the disciples were bold enough to ask for clarification. Thomas asked, "How do we know the way?" And Jesus's answer gave us that wonderful, foundational truth of salvation: "I am the way, and the truth, and the life; no one comes to the Father except through Me. If you had known Me, you would have known My Father also; from now on you know Him, and have seen Him" (vv. 5–7).

"Lord, show us the Father, and it is enough for us," Philip replied (v. 8). Jesus's response was a bit of a rebuke, but was also a blessing to Philip and to you and me today. Because in His answer, Jesus once again affirmed His unity with the Father: "The one who has seen Me has seen the Father" (v. 9).

So what we have seen in Jesus shows us who the Father is. But how does this relate to Jesus's perspective on the fruit of gentleness?

## *Gentle Jesus*

The Bible has much to say about the gentleness of Jesus, beginning in the Old Testament. In Matthew 12:18–21, Matthew quoted the prophet Isaiah:

> Behold, My Servant whom I have chosen;
> My Beloved in whom My soul delights;

> I will put My Spirit upon Him,
> And He will proclaim justice to the Gentiles.
> He will not quarrel, nor cry out;
> Nor will anyone hear His voice in the streets.
> A bent reed He will not break off,
> And a dimly burning wick He will not extinguish,
> Until He leads justice to victory.
> And in His name the Gentiles will hope.[1]

What did Isaiah mean by "a bent reed He will not break off, and a dimly burning wick He will not extinguish"? Both of these items have reached the end of their apparent usefulness. But instead of tossing them onto a garbage heap, the Messiah would deal gently with them. Both items represented people. Consider how Jesus responded to those whom the religious elite viewed as less-than: the physically limited, the spiritually oppressed, people enmeshed in immoral lifestyles, those lacking the ability to provide for their families as respected members of their society. Instead of casting them aside, Jesus reached out, imparting hope and wholeness.

Isaiah spoke of the Messiah's gentleness, and Jesus referred to Himself as gentle. In Matthew 11:28–29 we see a sweet invitation extended to those worn out by the world's cares. "Come to Me, all who are weary and burdened, and I will give you rest. Take My yoke upon you and learn from Me, for I am gentle and humble in heart, and you will find rest for your souls."

Finally, in 2 Corinthians 10:1, the apostle Paul prefaced his comments with an appeal to them "by the meekness and gentleness of Christ."

But what exactly is gentleness from a biblical standpoint?

## *Don't Be Mistaken*

A favorite scene of mine in the classic movie *The Princess Bride* includes a conversation between a character named Inigo Montoya and an archvillain. Throughout the film, Montoya hears the villain pronounce something as "inconceivable"—and each time, the inconceivable occurs. Montoya finally observes, "You keep using that word. I do not think it means what you think it means."[2]

Many of us make the same mistake when it comes to biblical gentleness, sometimes translated as "meekness." The ancient Greek word for gentleness, *praütēs*, does not mean what many of us think it does. Instead, the *Hebrew-Greek Key Word Study Bible* defines *praütēs* as "the result of a strong man's choice to control his reactions in submission to God. It is a balance born in strength of character stemming from confident trust in God, not from weakness or fear."[3] In other words, great strength under great control.

Steve Brown, founder of the Key Life Network, described it this way: "Meekness or gentleness is sensitivity to God. It is a power that causes a Christian to listen, to speak softly and to love genuinely. Meekness is not the opposite of strength; it is the opposite of unbridled angry, 'shooting from the hip.'"[4]

The prophet Isaiah painted a beautiful picture of God's gentleness—great strength under control—in 40:10–11:

> Behold, the Lord GOD will come with might,
> With His arm ruling for Him.
> Behold, His compensation is with Him,
> And His reward before Him.
> Like a shepherd He will tend His flock,
> In His arm He will gather the lambs
> And carry them in the fold of His robe;
> He will gently lead the nursing ewes.

The context of these verses describes the return of God's people from exile. The all-powerful God who rules over empires and nations, the one who executed judgment on Israel for their idolatry, would tenderly and gently regather His people.

This same great strength under great control was evident in the life of Jesus:

- Jesus rode into Jerusalem, "gentle and riding on a donkey" (Matthew 21:5 NIV), even though He knew that a mere five days later He would be cruelly executed.
- The Jesus who overturned money changers' tables in the temple out of zeal for His Father's house (Matthew 21:12–13) is the same Jesus who said to His Father, "I have come to do Your will" (Hebrews 10:9).
- The evening Jesus was betrayed, He surrendered to His Father's will when He said, "Father, if You are willing, remove this cup from Me; yet not My will, but Yours be done" (Luke 22:42).
- On that same evening, when Peter used his sword to injure the high priest's servant, Jesus said, "Put your sword back into its place. . . . Do you think that I cannot appeal to My Father, and He will at once put at My disposal more than twelve legions of angels? How then would the Scriptures be fulfilled, which say that it must happen this way?" (Matthew 26:52–54).

Don't be mistaken. Jesus was not a doormat. He was not weak. He had great strength under great control. And this characteristic of gentleness displayed by Jesus is the same fruit promised to every believer by the indwelling Holy Spirit.

## Recover and Grow

Years ago, when I first taught a Bible study on the fruit of the Spirit listed in Galatians 5:22–23, I ran into a problem. I stood in front of the attendees at the beginning of each class and introduced our topic: "Welcome to another session in our study of the fruit of the Spirit: love, joy, peace, patience, kindness, goodness, faithfulness, and self-control." I counted them off on raised fingers as I spoke, and ended with eight raised fingers each time. For the first few weeks I came up short by one. And it was always the same one: gentleness. I laughed it off at first, and my class laughed along with me until . . . one class member jokingly said maybe I kept forgetting gentleness because this was the display of fruit I needed to cultivate.

She said it with a smile, but the Holy Spirit used her humorous comment to get my attention. I tended to be task-oriented, focused on getting the job done. My natural emphasis was often on the project rather than the people involved—typical type A personality. An MBA and twenty years in the corporate world honed my project management skills. Give me a job to do and I got it done. Deliver results and get rewarded. Wall Street doesn't care about your—or anyone else's—feelings.

However, that's not God's way. Wall Street may not care, but God does. He used that conversation to remind me that people are more important than projects. Successful endeavors don't matter one bit if I leave a trail of hurting people in my wake. Yes, my goals may be important, but not as important as the people Jesus died to save. And in my desire to nurture gentleness as a fruit of the Spirit, I learned that the path to gentleness is found in submission.

## *Submission to the Father*

The biggest challenge to recovering and growing the fruit of gentleness is that we frequently view this fruit as less desirable than the other eight. We are not eager to cultivate a characteristic associated with weakness. And it doesn't help to know gentleness has also been defined as "patient submissiveness to offense"[5]—something we're rarely keen to do.

A huge part of the problem is that we try to cultivate a gentle spirit that can submit to offense without first submitting to our heavenly Father. No wonder we fail! As Jesus submitted to the will of His Father, we are called to follow His example. But in our Western, twenty-first-century culture, neither gentleness nor submission are viewed as attractive traits.

Jesus said, "Blessed are the gentle, for they will inherit the earth" (Matthew 5:5). But if we're honest, most of us don't want to wait for Jesus's second coming to receive the respect we believe we're due. We want it now. When we assert our rights, we are in effect telling God we'll submit to His authority and trust Him in other circumstances but not in this one. When someone offends us with their words or actions, our desire to put them in their place competes with our desire to surrender to the Holy Spirit's leading. And when we're mistreated and angrily fight for our rights, we communicate that submission was okay for Jesus, but it isn't for us. I can't speak for you, but for me, that's another big ouch!

The root of our reluctance to submit to God lies in the call of Jesus to His followers. In Matthew 16:24, "Jesus said to His disciples, 'If anyone wants to come after Me, he must deny himself, take up his cross, and follow Me.'" The apostle Paul understood this when he wrote, "I have been crucified with Christ; and it is no longer I who live, but Christ lives in me" (Galatians 2:20). This is dying to self. Surrendering my rights to myself—my agenda, my priorities, my life—and allowing God to use me as He chooses for my ultimate good and His eternal glory.

Denying our old desires and considering our old nature as dead is the foundation for nurturing the fruit of the Spirit, including the fruit of gentleness. Only then are we free to be equipped by the Holy Spirit to stand against the devil's schemes and temptations.

### *Responding to Satan's Schemes*

Earlier we explored the schemes that target a gentle spirit. When we surrender to the Holy Spirit and ask for His help, He provides what we need to stand against these temptations.

*Pride.* In 1 Peter 5:5–6, the apostle Peter noted, "God is opposed to the proud, but He gives grace to the humble. Therefore humble yourselves under the mighty hand of God, so that He may exalt you at the proper time." When we humble ourselves before God, we communicate trust in Him. Trust that He sovereignly acts on behalf of His children, allowing various circumstances to grow us into spiritual maturity.

Humility is also an antidote to being judgmental because it helps us view others from God's perspective. In Romans 5:6–8, Paul wrote:

> While we were still helpless, at the right time Christ died for the ungodly. For one will hardly die for a righteous person; though perhaps for the good person someone would even dare to die. But God demonstrates His own love toward us, in that while we were still sinners, Christ died for us.

God responded to our greatest need with love. He didn't beat us over the head with the law. Rather, He provided His Son, who was able to fully satisfy the law on our behalf. This doesn't mean we compromise truth or avoid all talk of hell. But as Paul wrote in Ephesians 4:15, we are to speak the truth in love. The great evangelist D. L. Moody is reported to have described it this way: "I must not preach hell unless I preach it with tears." Does the world see us gloating over their coming judgment, or do they see us sharing the way of escape in Jesus Christ with tears of gentle compassion in our eyes?

*Unconfessed sin.* Unconfessed sin has a way of cultivating hypocrisy instead of a gentle spirit. Oh, how superior I've felt judging someone else's sin! That is, until I read Romans 2:1, and the Holy Spirit convicted me to take the plank out of my own eye before I dared point out the speck in someone else's eye: "In that matter in which you judge someone else, you condemn yourself; for you who judge practice the same things."

God kindly provided the solution for this hypocrisy in 1 John 1:8–10:

> If we say that we have no sin, we are deceiving ourselves and the truth is not in us. If we confess our sins, He is faithful and righteous, so that He will forgive us our sins and cleanse us from all unrighteousness. If we say that we have not sinned, we make Him a liar and His word is not in us.

*Unforgiveness.* The pain of betrayal or other offenses can wound us both physically and emotionally. And if we've fallen for the devil's lies, we can find it difficult or nearly impossible to forgive. Instead, we deal harshly with the other person if we interact with them at all.

Still, the theme of forgiveness flows throughout the Bible. In Matthew 18:22, Jesus told Peter to forgive up to "seventy-seven times," a figurative way of saying, forgive until you lose count.

In Luke 7:47, Jesus said something that at first glance sounds a bit puzzling: "The one who is forgiven little, loves little." How does this apply to you and me? If we don't think we need much forgiveness, we won't extend much forgiveness either. But if we live with the daily—no, minute-by-minute—realization of how desperately we need God's forgiveness, we are moved to offer it to others with grateful hearts.

Paul connected gentleness with forgiveness in Colossians 3:12–13:

> As those who have been chosen of God, holy and beloved, put on a heart of compassion, kindness, humility, gentleness, and patience; bearing with one another, and forgiving each other, whoever has a complaint against anyone; just as the Lord forgave you, so must you do also.

Beyond forgiveness, Paul also added the importance of gently restoring the one who is forgiven.[6] Forgiveness flows from cultivating gentleness, and gentleness flows from cultivating forgiveness.

*Worry.* Gentleness with others is a difficult challenge when we direct our attention inward. Thankfully, Jesus provided the solution to eliminating the inward focus that gives birth to worry and fear. In His Sermon on the Mount, He gave a straightforward command in Matthew 6:25: "Do not be worried." That sounds easier said than done, doesn't it? But once again, for every command in the Bible, there are also instructions on how to obey.

No matter how hard we try not to worry, unsettling thoughts have a way of creeping back in. So Jesus did not stop with a command telling us what *not* to do. He told us how to replace those thoughts. Jesus said, "Seek first [God's] kingdom and His righteousness, and all these things will be provided to you" (v. 33). Seeking God's kingdom redirects our focus outward to how and where God is at work. And a characteristic of His kingdom is the fruit of gentleness.

*Uncontrolled tongue.* Remember the verses from Proverbs about the tongue in the first section of this chapter? Did you notice how each one involved a comparison? Let's consider them again:

There is one who speaks rashly like the thrusts of a sword,
But the tongue of the wise brings healing.
(12:18)

A gentle answer turns away wrath,
But a harsh word stirs up anger.
(15:1)

A soothing tongue is a tree of life,
But perversion in it crushes the spirit.
(15:4)

Death and life are in the power of the tongue.
(18:21)

That last line, contrasting death and life, sums it up. Our words can have a powerful impact for either good or evil. And whether we like it or not, our words reveal our hearts. So being more gentle with our words begins with examining our spirit. And that brings us back to our submission to the Holy Spirit.

Jesus displayed great strength under great control. We can do the same only as we submit to His Spirit. True submission yields the power to be gentle when every fiber of our being screams for us to further our own interests regardless of others' needs or feelings.

## Share the Harvest

I recently visited a friend after the birth of her second child. As her three-year-old son eagerly reached out to touch his new baby brother, she cautioned, "Be gentle!"

We often promote gentleness when dealing with people, events, or items we view as fragile. Babies. China dinnerware and crystal glasses. Special occasions. But for some people, "gentle" is nothing more than a setting on their washing machine. It has no place in their human interactions.

Our reluctance to appear as doormats is a great obstacle to sharing the fruit of gentleness. Those who stand up for their rights are respected more than those who defer to others. We want to be served more than we want to serve. Jesus turns that attitude on its head.

## *Servanthood*

Since Jesus modeled gentleness—great strength under great control—so effectively, let's explore how we can learn from His example. It starts with servanthood. To see how, let's revisit Isaiah 42:1–4 (quoted earlier in Matthew):

> Behold, My Servant, whom I uphold;
> My chosen one in whom My soul delights.
> I have put My Spirit upon Him;
> He will bring forth justice to the nations.
> He will not cry out nor raise His voice,
> Nor make His voice heard in the street.
> A bent reed He will not break off
> And a dimly burning wick He will not extinguish;
> He will faithfully bring forth justice.
> He will not be disheartened or crushed
> Until He has established justice on the earth;
> And the coastlands will wait expectantly for His law.

Isaiah introduced the Messiah's gentleness by saying, "Here is my servant" (NIV). The gentle qualities of the Savior were founded on His full submission to His Father's plans and purposes. Just as Jesus dealt gently with those considered less-than in His culture, His followers are to do the same. It has been said that the best test of servanthood is if I act like a servant when I'm treated like one. For many people, servanthood is an even less popular concept than gentleness!

## *Practical Applications*

When a friend asked how I would describe the apostle Paul, the first word that came to my mind was not *gentle*. It's not even the tenth or twentieth word. Yet variations of the word *gentle* appear again and again in Paul's letters to the early church. In his instructions in Ephesians 4:1–4, Paul even listed gentleness as a characteristic that cultivates unity in the body of Christ.

Paul gave similar instructions to the church in Philippi: "Let your gentle spirit be known to all people" (Philippians 4:5). And in his leadership instructions to Timothy, Paul exhorted his protégé to "pursue righteousness, godliness, faith, love, perseverance, and gentleness" (1 Timothy 6:11). Similarly, he told Titus, "Remind them . . . to be gentle" (Titus 3:1–2).

Gentleness is an important mark of the body of Christ. So what does being a gentle servant look like in practical terms for you and me?

### *Watching What We Say*

Hearts that regularly pursue intimacy with the Lord will consistently speak gently to others. The earliest science experiment I recall from elementary school reminds me of this truth. We placed cut celery stalks in jars containing water dyed with food coloring. As if by magic, the various colors traveled through the celery as the stalk absorbed the water.

Similarly, the Holy Spirit's gentleness will flow through us as we submit to Him. So when our words are harsh or insensitive, that's a clue regarding our level of intimacy with the Lord, and a reminder to spend additional time for His Spirit to show us areas we need to resubmit to Him. He won't be surprised by what we bring Him. Remember what King David wrote in Psalm 139:4: "Even before there is a word on my tongue, behold, LORD, You know it all."

Even when I'm careful about using gentle words, I still find a need to regularly ask the Lord to "set a guard . . . over my mouth" (Psalm 141:3). I desire, as James 1:19 wisely counsels me, to be quick to listen and slow to speak.

### *Silence*

There is power in learning when to speak and when to be silent. The writer of Proverbs 10:19 understood this: "When words are many, transgression is not lacking, but whoever restrains his lips is prudent" (ESV). Such a convicting reminder for me! The more I speak, the greater the probability I'll later regret something I've said.

Of course, we can't forget Solomon's wisdom in Ecclesiastes 3:1, 7: "There is an appointed time for everything. And there is a time for every matter under heaven. . . . A time to be silent and a time to speak." Jesus modeled that wisdom. He spoke up unhesitatingly and forcefully to the religious leaders: "Woe to you, scribes and Pharisees, hypocrites! . . . You blind guides . . . !" (Matthew 23:23–24). Yet when He was on trial before Pontius Pilate, Matthew 26:63 tells us Jesus kept silent. Even Pilate was amazed Jesus did not answer any of the charges made against Him (27:14). Why would Jesus speak up in one place and not another? Timing. God's plan of salvation necessitated Jesus's illegal conviction and death. Speaking up in self-defense during the trials was not part of the plan.

Learning when to speak and when to remain silent is not easy. Perhaps that's why Elisabeth Elliot's prayer resonates with me so much:

> Lord, deliver me from the urge to open my mouth when I should shut it. Give me the wisdom to keep silence where silence is wise. Remind me that not everything needs to be said, and that there are very few things that need to be said by me.[7]

### *Evangelism and Discipleship*

When I took my boxer, Duke, for walks, trying to drag him by his leash where he didn't want to go usually led to a battle of our wills. And pushing a ninety-pound boxer wasn't even an option. Our most effective and enjoyable walks occurred when he willingly walked beside me.

Evangelism and discipleship operate on the same principle. It's not helpful to attempt to push or pull people into spiritual growth. Instead, effective discipleship occurs when we gently walk alongside them.

The apostle Peter addressed this when he wrote, "Always be prepared to give an answer to everyone who asks you to give the reason for the hope that you have. But do this with gentleness and respect" (1 Peter 3:15 NIV). And Paul, modeling discipleship among the early Thessalonian believers, reminded them, "We were gentle among you, like a nursing mother taking care of her own children" (1 Thessalonians 2:7 ESV).

We can easily fall into the trap of expecting other Christians to grow at the same spiritual pace as us, but every person is unique. Gentle discipleship displays the fruit of the Spirit as we welcome others into the body of Christ.

### *Responding to Conflict*

Relational conflict has been around since the very first family, when Cain killed his brother, Abel. Still, it seems as if people are more easily triggered than ever before. And when people are triggered, they don't respond, they react, often with deep-seated emotion.

As Christians, we can allow the unrighteousness around us to make us so angry that our reactions are no different from the way unbelievers react to conflict. But if people can't tell the difference between believers and unbelievers, why should they listen to what we say about the gospel?

You might think our culture has so firmly rejected God that we can no longer be gentle if we want to restore righteousness. However, consider the world Christians lived in during the first century. An idolatrous society? The gods of the Roman pantheon numbered in the hundreds. An immoral culture? The level of sexual immorality in ancient Rome would make even unbelievers blush today.

Yet amid that blatantly unrighteous culture, the apostle Paul told Titus, "Remind the people to be subject to rulers and authorities, to be obedient, to be ready to do whatever is good, to slander no one, to be peaceable and considerate, and always to be gentle toward everyone" (Titus 3:1–2 NIV). Did you catch Paul's inclusion of gentleness?

From Proverbs 15:1, which tells us, "A gentle answer turns away wrath," to Paul's admonition to Timothy to correct opponents with gentleness,[8] this fruit of the Spirit is needed as much today as ever before in responding to conflict.

Although gentleness may be the most overlooked and least sought of all the fruit, the Holy Spirit inspired Paul to list it with the rest. Let's not dismiss gentleness as unimportant, because this characteristic enables us to be more like Christ. Thankfully, we're not left on our own to develop it. It's the Holy Spirit's fruit, and cultivating it is accomplished in our submission to Him.

## APPLICATION QUESTIONS

1. Which of the five schemes of the devil (pride, unconfessed sin, unforgiveness, worry, uncontrolled tongue) are you most vulnerable to regarding the fruit of gentleness?
2. When you think of God, does the characteristic of gentleness spring to mind? Why or why not?
3. How does the biblical definition of gentleness differ from the way our culture defines it today?
4. How does seeing the gentleness modeled by Jesus change how you view God the Father?
5. Why do you think submission to the Holy Spirit is so critically linked to the fruit of gentleness?
6. Consider the five approaches to standing against Satan's schemes and recovering the fruit of gentleness. Which do you think will be most helpful to you? Why?
7. Were you surprised by how often the Bible encourages gentleness? Which area linked to gentleness surprised you the most? Why?
8. How might God be calling you to express gentleness in serving others this week?

9. When you are disrespected or angry, what do your words reveal about your relationship with Christ? What might need to change?
10. What did you think about Elisabeth Elliot's prayer regarding silence? How easy is it for you to remain silent in the face of conflict or adversity?

## CHAPTER 10

# The Discipline of Our Fruit Is Self-Control

Of the previous eight displays of the fruit of the Spirit, every description we explored focused on their source: the Holy Spirit. This makes the name of this final demonstration of the Spirit's fruit especially unusual: self-control. Self-control. *Self*-control.

Why would the Holy Spirit, through the apostle Paul, include the word *self* in the name of this fruit? To find the answer, let's dig in to this final facet of the precious fruit of God's Holy Spirit.

## Recognize the Enemy's Tactics

Self-control and discipline are fast becoming foreign concepts in our Western society. The prevailing consensus leans toward a philosophy of "If it feels good, do it!" Our culture demands freedom to fulfill every desire without consequences.

Satan uses the desires of our flesh to distract us from acknowledging responsibility for the results. The devil baits hooks and sets traps, all for the purpose of tempting us to stumble. The letter of James in the New Testament contains a vivid word picture of this. Let's take time to unpack the original language of chapter 1, verse 14: "Each one is tempted when he is carried away and enticed by his own lust." The Greek word for "carried away" (some translations say "dragged away"), *exelkō,* means "to draw out." It's a hunting metaphor to describe how wild game is lured out of hiding into a trap.[1] The Greek word for "enticed," *deleazō*, is a fishing term for the use of bait.[2]

So what is the bait with which we are enticed and drawn away? Our own lust (some translations use the word *desires*). We want what we want, and we're willing to leave the protective boundaries of self-control to get it. Our vulnerabilities include selfishness, unbridled emotions, the blame game, and dismantled boundaries.

## *Selfishness*

Every person is born with a predisposition to selfishness. Young children are taught to share, but they never have to be taught to be selfish. Almost as soon as they learn to speak, they are quick to respond with a loud "Mine!" to protect toys, snacks, or their turn on the playground swings. We're all born with a sin nature, and selfishness is its inherent fruit.

It would be nice if we naturally outgrew the tendency to satisfy selfish impulses—a tendency that consistently works against self-control. But if we could, we wouldn't need the Holy Spirit to cultivate this fruit.

Instead, we buy into the devil's lies: What's right for you doesn't have to be right for me. If it feels good, do it. Life is short—no need to wait to gratify your desires.

The enemy does not want us to know that, according to Galatians 6:8, indulging our fleshly desires leads to destruction.

Gratifying our selfish desires is not a new temptation. Consider the apostle Paul's interaction two thousand years ago with the Roman Governor Felix in Acts 24:24–25:

> Some days later Felix arrived with Drusilla his wife, who was Jewish, and he sent for Paul and heard him speak about faith in Christ Jesus. But as he was discussing righteousness, self-control, and the judgment to come, Felix became frightened and responded, "Go away for now, and when I have an opportunity, I will summon you."

Did you catch the reference to self-control? In the first century, the pagan Roman culture had deteriorated into a culture of immorality and excess. Self-control was not a popular concept. History tells us Drusilla divorced her husband to become Felix's third wife. She and Felix believed they could do what they wanted, when they wanted, without regard to self-control.[3] When Paul included self-control along with righteousness and coming judgment, that was enough to strike fear into the governor's heart.

### *Unbridled Emotions*

Early in my marriage, we owned a car that developed an intermittent electrical problem causing it to die while being driven. If you've ever dealt with an electrical issue in older vehicles, you know it can be difficult to resolve. We brought the car in for servicing on several occasions, but the technicians could not locate the problem. One day while we were driving, the car died once again. After we coasted to the side of the road, my husband got out and gave full vent to his anger and frustration, forcefully kicking the side of the car. Again we had the car towed in for servicing—and this time the technicians found the problem: a small loose wire. Fixing it cost three times less than repairing the rear side quarter panel Russ kicked in. For years afterward, Russ said he would never forget this lesson in handling anger.

Our culture has bought the enemy's lie that it's not only okay to give full vent to our emotions, it's beneficial. We'll feel better if we let it all hang out. But doing so can damage relationships, sometimes permanently. Many of us have experienced broken relationships because we spewed our anger on another person, or they spewed their anger on us. So we learn a lesson: It's not okay to explode our emotions on others.

There's an opposite extreme, though. In our efforts to be "good Christians," we may bury emotions such as anger or frustration so far down that they smolder deep within us. A volcano of bitterness and resentment builds over months and years until we can no longer hold back the emotional explosion. Or we stuff our need to emotionally connect with others because we've been hurt in the past and don't want to experience that pain again. Those emotions remain locked inside us, isolating us from the healthy relationships God intends us to experience.

### *The Blame Game*

Have you ever participated in a bucket brigade? You've probably seen one in the movies or on television. It's composed of people lined up to put out a fire by passing buckets of water down the line, from the water source to the fire.

While I've never passed the bucket in a bucket brigade, I'm sorry to say I have experience in "passing the buck" after making a poor choice. The practice has been around for thousands of years, beginning in the garden of Eden. In that perfect environment, Adam and Eve did a great imitation of a fire brigade line, only instead of passing buckets of water, they passed buckets of blame.

Genesis 3:6 tells us, "When [Eve] saw that the tree was good for food, and that it was a delight to the eyes, and that the tree was desirable to make one wise, she took some of its fruit and ate; and she also gave some to her husband with her, and he ate." Regardless of God's prohibitions, they wanted what they wanted. The blame game began when God called Adam and Eve to accountability. It started with Adam: "The woman whom You gave to be with me, she gave me some of the fruit of the tree, and I ate" (v. 12). Then Eve, who said in verse 13, "The serpent deceived me, and I ate." (By the way, did you notice that Adam blamed God as well as Eve? "The woman whom *You* gave to be with me"—a brazen insinuation!)

We're not much different today. After all, it's not our fault if we fall victim to someone else's influence, is it? So we come up with excuses. The devil made me do it. Or our ethnicity. Or our family heritage. *They're* responsible for our trigger temper, unhealthy eating habits, or immoral choices.

### *Dismantled Boundaries*

Though it's a century old, the song "Don't Fence Me In" echoes today's culture. We don't want to be told what to do. Don't fence me in with marriage vows or the gender God created me to be. Don't fence me in with truthfulness if telling a "harmless" lie will make life a little easier. Don't fence me in with talk about eternal judgment when I just want to enjoy today.

Satan tempts us to view God's boundaries as harshly restrictive, keeping something good from us. Remember what he told Eve in the garden when she expressed concern about God's warning? "You certainly will not die! For God knows that on the day you eat from it your eyes will be opened, and you will become like God, knowing good and evil" (Genesis 3:4–5).

The more the devil can tempt us to view God as a cosmic killjoy, the easier it is for us to disregard God's boundaries. And Satan is sly enough to start with seemingly small temptations. Cut a corner here. Tell a white lie there. Withhold forgiveness because everyone knows that person doesn't deserve it. Help yourself to office supplies—everyone does it. Give the sales clerk a tongue-lashing because she disrespected you—after all, it's important to stand up for yourself and defend your rights.

Whether through selfishness, unbridled emotions, the blame game, or dismantled boundaries, we are surrounded by countless temptations to excuse our lack of self-control. But what does God have to say about this fruit?

## Nurture a Right Perspective

The nine displays of the fruit of the Spirit in every Christian's life are also attributes of God. And yes, God's attributes include self-control! Don't believe me? Check out Isaiah 42:14: "I have kept silent for a long time, I have kept still and restrained Myself." Everything God does is perfect, including His timing. Yet once again our perspective of this fruit often differs from God's.

### *Our Ways*

We think God can be as capricious as the ancient mythological gods. His anger might burst forth unpredictably, or He may work according to an incomprehensible timetable that makes no sense to us.

### *God's Ways*

God wants us to know that people can be impulsive, but He is not. People can act hastily, but God does not. Consider His great plan of salvation: "When the fullness of the time came, God sent His Son" (Galatians 4:4).

Even God's anger and judgment are always controlled. At least one hundred years passed from the time God told Noah about the coming flood to when it actually occurred. And consider Nineveh. God could have destroyed that evil capital city of Assyria in a moment, yet He sent the prophet Jonah with a warning to repent. They did, temporarily, and God withheld His wrath at the time. Not until one hundred years after Jonah did the prophet Nahum again proclaim judgment against Nineveh.

Time and again God warned His own people of judgment for their idolatry and faithlessness. For two hundred years, God sent His prophets to warn the northern kingdom of Israel and the southern kingdom of Judah. Both received the same message: Repent and turn back to the one true, living God. After two centuries, God finally allowed the Assyrian Empire to take Israel into captivity. Judah met a similar fate 140 years later when the Babylonian Empire conquered them. Even then God's judgment was measured and controlled, waiting hundreds of years before its fulfillment and then, for Judah, limited their exile to seventy years of Babylonian captivity.

Self-control is a key aspect of God's character. Now let's explore what the Lord has to say about self-control for you and me.

### *The Walls of Self-Control*

How important is this fruit of the Spirit? Proverbs 25:28 says, "Like a city whose walls are broken through is a person who lacks self-control" (NIV).

To grasp the importance of this description, we need to appreciate the significance of city walls in biblical times. Walls are mentioned more than 150 times in the Bible. An entire book of the Bible, Nehemiah, focuses on rebuilding the wall around Jerusalem after the exile. At the end of the seventy years of captivity, Nehemiah obtained permission from the Persian king to leave the court and return to Jerusalem. He had one purpose: restoration of the city wall.

In ancient times, high walls of stones or bricks formed a defensive barricade against attack.[4] According to *The Archaeological Study Bible*, "A city whose walls were broken down was considered defenseless and disgraced."[5] And so it is with self-control: Without its protective benefits, we too are defenseless against our enemy's tactics.

## *The Holy Spirit Frees Us*

Freedom. We seek it. We treasure it. And we struggle against anything we perceive as restricting our freedom. So isn't it interesting that the apostle Paul included the fruit of the Spirit—particularly self-control—in a portion of his letter dedicated to the subject of freedom?

Before I began writing this book, I don't think I ever associated self-control or walls with freedom. Yet as I researched the fifth chapter of Paul's letter to the Galatian church, those relationships became clear. Galatians 5, the same chapter in which Paul listed the fruit of the Spirit, includes a clear theme of freedom. Consider these verses:

- v. 1: "It was for freedom that Christ set us free; therefore keep standing firm and do not be subject again to a yoke of slavery."
- v. 13: "You were called to freedom, brothers and sisters; only do not turn your freedom into an opportunity for the flesh, but serve one another through love."
- vv. 16, 18: "I say, walk by the Spirit, and you will not carry out the desire of the flesh. . . . If you are led by the Spirit, you are not under the Law."
- vv. 22–23: "The fruit of the Spirit is love, joy, peace, patience, kindness, goodness, faithfulness, gentleness, self-control; against such things there is no law."

Self-control frees us to live without guilt and regret. It enables us to reflect Christ in all we say and do. Paul concluded in verse 25: "If we live by the Spirit, let's follow the Spirit as well." Isn't this what the fruit of the Spirit is all about? Keeping in step with the Spirit. Being sensitive to His promptings. Obeying His Word. Saying no to the demands and impulses of the flesh that work against our freedom in Christ. In other words, self-control.

### *The Holy Spirit Equips Us*

Throughout this book, we've explored the relationship between relying on the Holy Spirit's equipping and our own intentional efforts. This critical balance is especially evident in the fruit of self-control. In his letter to Timothy, Paul reminded Timothy that God had given believers in Christ "a spirit not of fear but of power and love and self-control" (2 Timothy 1:7 ESV). Some translations say *self-discipline* or simply *discipline* in place of self-control.

We cannot serve God as clean vessels apart from the power of the Holy Spirit active in our lives. He gives us the desire to live a life pleasing to God *and* the ability to follow through on that desire. Do we apply our efforts to do so? Yes. But the fuel for those efforts is sourced in acknowledging our weakness and the Holy Spirit's power. Elisabeth Elliot wrote, "Humanity for us . . . means both dependence and obedience."[6]

Where does love fit into this? The first display of fruit we explored is love. And it's only fitting we come full circle to examine how love affects our desire and ability to die to self. Dying to self requires that we love someone or something more than ourselves. Selfishness is wrapped up in furthering our own interests and prioritizing our own agendas. But remember what Jesus identified as the greatest command in Matthew 22:37–39: "'You shall love the Lord your God with all your heart, and with all your soul, and with all your mind.' This is the great and foremost commandment. The second is like it, 'You shall love your neighbor as yourself.'"

First John 4:19 reminds us, "We love, because He first loved us." Our ability to love God and anyone else other than ourselves is a gift from the indwelling Holy Spirit. Our grateful response is to act on this love by setting aside our selfish priorities.

So God has given us a spirit not only of power and love but also of self-control, or self-discipline. Second Timothy 1:7 is clear: God has *given* us these things, including self-control. We are equipped to exercise self-discipline by the power of the Holy Spirit and a motive that flows from love.

### Soldiers of the Cross

Soldiers serving in the military grasp, better than most people, the importance of self-discipline. They live life at the direction of their commanding officer. The apostle Paul understood the parallels of military life to the Christian life when he wrote, "No soldier in active service entangles himself in the affairs of everyday life, so that he may please the one who enlisted him" (2 Timothy 2:4). Elisabeth Elliot summed it up this way: "Discipline is not my claim on Christ, but the evidence of His claim on me."[7]

James 4:7 also conveys a military association. "Submit therefore to God. But resist the devil, and he will flee from you." The military connection is found in the Greek word for "submit." *Hupotasso* is formed from the prefix *hupo,* which means "under," and *tassō,* a word that "originally carried the military connotation of drawing up troops (or ships) into battle array."[8] So *hupotassō* means to place under in an orderly manner. For Christians, self-control or self-discipline involves arranging our lives under the Holy Spirit as soldiers arrange their lives in military ranks under their commanding officers.

With all this in mind from God's perspective, how do we then recover the fruit of self-control?

## Recover and Grow

Many Christians naturally approach self-control by simply trying harder. But the fruit of self-control flourishes best when we learn to die to ourselves.

Few, if any, of us like to think about dying and death. What's comforting to me about death is the promise of heaven—being in the presence of God—and the assurance of reunion with loved ones who were Christians. But even with the certainty of heaven, often the greater fear is not death but the *process* of dying.

I can't begin to count the number of people who have told me,

"When it's time for me to go, I hope I die peacefully in my sleep." While we understand life will end for all of us, we fear the possibility of a painful process. Or we fear the humbling helplessness of being captive in a hospital bed while connected to assorted machines.

How is this associated with recovering the fruit of self-control?

Self-control is directly related to dying to self, or as Jesus said, denying self. And yes, the dying process can be painful and humbling. We wish the command to deny ourselves could be as painless as falling asleep and waking up with all those selfish desires wiped away. Instead, dying to self requires us to be intentional.

Jesus said, "If anyone wants to come after Me, he must deny himself, take up his cross daily, and follow Me" (Luke 9:23). How do we deny ourselves? The apostle Paul answered this when he wrote in Romans 6:11, "Consider yourselves to be dead to sin, but alive to God in Christ Jesus." And in his letter to the Galatian church, Paul wrote, "I have been crucified with Christ; and it is no longer I who live, but Christ lives in me; and the life which I now live in the flesh I live by faith in the Son of God, who loved me and gave Himself up for me" (Galatians 2:20). These are all important verses, but how do we apply them on a daily basis?

Our relationship with God through Christ is one of both life and death. Through the gift of salvation we exchange our sin for Christ's righteousness, our plans for God's purposes, and our good for God's best. We release our desired right to be in charge and instead surrender to the lordship of our sovereign heavenly Father. Dying to self describes the reality of treating our old nature as dead. If it's dead, then the call of our old way of life no longer has power over us. We are free to live in the power of the resurrected life Christ purchased for us and offers to us.

## *Connect the Dots or Instant Discipline?*

When I was a kid, I loved coloring books that contained connect-the-dot pictures. Those pictures were a bonus: two activities on one page. I would connect the numbered dots and then color in the picture. But the picture did not make sense if I failed to connect the dots in order.

Leaving even one number unaccounted for or out of order left me with an incomplete or distorted image.

When I read the apostle Peter's description of spiritual growth, I'm reminded of those connect-the-dot coloring books from years ago. In this passage, he included a methodical list of steps, starting with faith and ending with love:

> Make every effort to add to your faith goodness; and to goodness, knowledge; and to knowledge, self-control; and to self-control, perseverance; and to perseverance, godliness; and to godliness, mutual affection; and to mutual affection, love. (2 Peter 1:5–7 NIV)

Eight components that—in the order listed—build a framework for solid spiritual growth. Two points in particular struck me about this list. First, it's structured like a ladder, with each characteristic building on the one that came before. And second, did you notice the position of self-control? Self-control is planted smack in the middle of the list. It anchors the previous three characteristics while forming a solid foundation for the following four qualities.

Let's unpack this passage as it relates to the fruit of the Spirit.

*Adding the building blocks of a godly life.* Peter introduced the building blocks of spiritual maturity with the admonishment to "make every effort." The believers were to do their utmost to add each building block he was about to name.

The first block, faith, is foundational: "Add to your faith . . ." Commentator Kenneth O. Gangel wrote, "Faith in Jesus Christ is what separates Christians from all other people. *Pistis,* trust in the Savior which brings one into the family of God, is the foundation of all other qualities in the Christian life."[9] Our relationship with the Father is founded on faith in what Christ did for us, not faith in what we can do for Him.

Added to faith is goodness, otherwise known as moral excellence. Christians are motivated to be and do good because of our faith in Christ. Next comes knowledge. By itself, knowledge only puffs us up.

But built on the foundation of faith and goodness, seeking spiritual truth draws us into greater intimacy with the Lord as we get to know Him through His Word.

That brings us to self-control. As we grow in faith, goodness, and knowledge, these qualities equip us to control our passions and responses to people and situations. And related to self-control is the next building block: perseverance. The discipline of self-control does not happen in an instant. Habits that took years to become embedded in our lives need to be replaced with new habits by the power of the Holy Spirit. Godliness, affection, and love are then added to this list of character qualities.

It's not a coincidence that self-control is sandwiched between knowledge and perseverance. As we submit to the Holy Spirit, the more we learn about God and ourselves through the Bible, the more we will be equipped to "keep on keeping on."

*Training in self-control.* As we continue to explore the long-term perspective needed for cultivating self-control, we see comparisons to physical training in Scripture. In 1 Corinthians 9:24–27, Paul pointed to himself as an example:

> Do you not know that those who run in a race all run, but only one receives the prize? Run in such a way that you may win. Everyone who competes in the games exercises self-control in all things. So they do it to obtain a perishable wreath, but we an imperishable. Therefore I run in such a way as not to run aimlessly; I box in such a way, as to avoid hitting air; but I strictly discipline my body and make it my slave, so that, after I have preached to others, I myself will not be disqualified.

Olympic athletes lay aside every other distraction so they can commit fully to training for the prize. We are called to do the same, but our prize is an eternal crown, not a perishable wreath. It's the same mindset as earlier in Romans 12:1, where Paul urged us to offer our bodies "as a living and holy sacrifice, acceptable to God" as an act of true worship.

So what does this look like, especially applied to those vulnerable areas the devil targets to tempt us? Let's examine them from God's perspective.

*Cultivating selflessness.* Combating selfishness is not as easy as changing clothes. Yet that's the image Paul used to illustrate the importance of changing our perspective, "put[ting] on the new self," which is God-focused, not self-absorbed:

> You were taught, with regard to your former way of life, to put off your old self, which is being corrupted by its deceitful desires; to be made new in the attitude of your minds; and to put on the new self, created to be like God in true righteousness and holiness. (Ephesians 4:22–24 NIV)

Paul referred to this transformation in Romans 12:2: "Do not be conformed to this world, but be transformed by the renewing of your mind, so that you may prove what the will of God is, that which is good and acceptable and perfect." We accomplish this renewal by spending time reading, studying, memorizing, and applying God's Word to replace the world's influence on our thoughts. When Jesus prayed for His followers, He asked His Father to sanctify them—to set them apart from the world—in the truth of His Word. This request was not only for His disciples two thousand years ago, it was for you and me today.[10] Paul wrote, "Set your minds on the things that are above, not on the things that are on earth" (Colossians 3:2). And Peter also stressed the importance of God's Word when he wrote, "You have been born again . . . through the living and enduring word of God" (1 Peter 1:23). Why such emphasis on spending intentional time in God's Word? My own experience has revealed that the world influences my perspective more than I might realize. And self-examination is inadequate unless I compare my thoughts to a standard outside myself: the standard of God's Word.

*Finding the right place for our emotions.* Self-control involves controlling our emotions instead of being led by them. The danger here is in thinking we have to get rid of our emotions. Nothing could be further from the truth. God created us as emotional beings. Emotions are not sinful in themselves; uncontrolled, however, they open the door to sin.

Elisabeth Elliot advises,

> Do not try to fortify yourself against emotions. Recognize them; name them, if that helps; and then lay them open before the Lord for His training of your responses. The discipline of emotions is the training of responses.[11]

*Taking responsibility and accountability.* Ditching the blame game requires practicing responsibility and accountability. And the first step is to stop making excuses. After a failure, most of us have at one time or another used the excuse "I'm only human!" That's true, but as Christians we are no longer controlled by our old nature. As Paul wrote in 2 Corinthians 5:17, "If anyone is in Christ, this person is a new creation; the old things passed away; behold, new things have come."

Author Britt Mooney explores this combination of responsibility and accountability:

> There are some things God will not give us from the community of faith. We only get them from him directly. There are other things God will not give us alone. We only get them from the gathering of the believers and their spiritual gifts. . . . The body of Christ, when operating as it should, also spurs us on to greater commitment and personal discipline, encouraging us in our gifts and helping us when we momentarily fail. This is what family does. In doing so, we prepare ourselves and each other for the mission ahead.[12]

There are no lone rangers in the body of Christ. We need accountability to Christ and to each other!

*Valuing fences.* Do we value fences or fight against them?

I have an invisible fence around my yard. Invisible in the sense that it's an electric wire buried six inches underground. The "fence" transmitter emitted a radio signal calibrated to my dogs' collars. If the dogs ventured too close to the boundary, they received a small electric charge. When we first installed the fence, the dogs chafed at the restriction. But I knew something they couldn't understand: freedom to run beyond the fence into the street could have deadly consequences. After a few weeks, they didn't notice the restriction. Instead, they freely ran and chased each other with abandon within the boundaries that kept them safe.

When God says don't, do we chafe at the restriction? Do we doubt His goodness as Eve did in the garden, thinking God is withholding something good? Or do we say, like the psalmist in Psalm 119:14–16: "I have rejoiced in the way of Your testimonies. . . . I will meditate on Your precepts. . . . I shall delight in Your statutes"?

As we recover and cultivate the fruit of self-control, we become better able to share it. What might it look like to do so?

## Share the Harvest

Displaying self-control is not something that helps cultivate this fruit in others—or is it? We may not be able to "give" self-control to someone else, but we can model this character quality. The problem is, how can we exemplify something we're struggling to apply ourselves?

Have you failed at self-control with a habit so often that you feel there's no point in even trying anymore? Fear that you'll never get it right? Have you experienced failures that cause you to doubt your ability to be a witness for Christ to others? Do the breaches in your walls of self-control cause you to isolate from other Christians to prevent them from learning of your weaknesses?

The apostle Peter may have been responding to these concerns among believers when he wrote, "[God's] divine power has granted to us everything pertaining to life and godliness, through the true knowledge of Him who called us by His own glory and excellence"

(2 Peter 1:3). Did you catch that? By the power of His Holy Spirit, our heavenly Father has given us *everything* we need to live a godly life.

And that's precisely what the devil wants us to forget. Because if we forget we have everything we need to live a godly life, then we'll run away from God's call to live in authentic community with other believers.

So how do we "share" self-control in practical ways despite our own struggles without being hypocrites?

### *Release the Illusion of Control*

I am a self-confessed recovering control freak. In my ongoing recovery, I am repeatedly reminded, as we saw in an earlier chapter, that control is nothing more than an illusion. If we struggle to control ourselves, why would we ever think we can control other situations or people?

The question of the day is, *Am I consistently practicing the habit of letting go of my attempts to control?* As God keeps teaching me (yes, I'm a slow learner!), I was never really in control. God is sovereign, ruling over everything; I am not. If I truly believe this, I will choose to replace my attempts to control people and situations with trust in our omniscient, omnipresent, and omnipotent heavenly Father.

How is this related to sharing the fruit of self-control? The answer is in community. Mere talk about self-control carries the message only so far. But when we model self-control before others rather than trying to control them, its power is undeniable.

### *Authenticity*

Ever have someone ask you how you're doing, and you answered, "Fine"? That wouldn't be a problem if it were true. But what about when you are so far from fine that one more question will drive you over the edge to drown in an ocean of tears?

Many Christians confuse the fruit of self-control with stoicism. Stoicism includes enduring suffering without displaying emotion—the "I'm fine" response when we're falling apart inside. But the answer to out-of-control emotions is not to deny they exist.

Such stoicism does much damage to the cause of Christ. Unbelievers see through our masks and conclude we are hypocrites, lying to ourselves and others. No one is ever "fine" every minute of every day. Who would want to join such a phony group? But worse yet, other Christians—especially new ones—may actually believe the lie. Because they *don't* feel fine all the time, they may conclude they're failing in their faith. And they too put up a facade.

This doesn't mean we should unload a thirty-minute, detailed description of all our troubles when we greet an acquaintance in the grocery store's frozen food aisle. But it's important to be authentic. That's why it's valuable to be part of a small group—a circle of trusted believers in whom we can confide. And it's okay to let unbelieving friends know when we're facing difficulties. When we allow others to see us handling trouble by faith in Christ, our authenticity may create a hunger in them for faith and strength to respond to their own troubles.

### *Respond Versus React*

If ever there was an impetuous person in the Bible, the apostle Peter would be first in line for the title. Self-control was not a character quality that came naturally to this rough-and-ready fisherman. Peter was one of those people who frequently forgot to "engage brain before putting mouth in gear." For example:

- In Matthew 16:21–22, when Jesus told His disciples of His coming suffering and death, Peter rebuked Him, saying, "God forbid it, Lord! This shall never happen to You!"
- In Mark 9:5, Peter was one of three disciples Jesus brought up a mountain to witness His transfiguration and the appearance of Elijah and Moses. Once again, Peter spoke without thinking when he suggested they build three shelters, one each for Jesus, Moses, and Elijah. How do we know Peter spoke impetuously? Because the gospel writer notes in verse 6, "For he did not know how to reply; for they became terrified."
- And in John 18:10, we see Peter in the garden of Gethsemane when Judas betrayed Jesus. Peter reacted by drawing his sword and cutting off the ear of the high priest's servant.

Peter was a prime example to us of how *not* to share the fruit of self-control. Yet his time with Jesus transformed him. Only then could he later write, "Make every effort to add to your faith . . . self-control" (2 Peter 1:5–6 NIV). Peter offered a helpful illustration of the difference between responding and reacting.

We share self-control when we submit to the Holy Spirit's transformative power. Others are blessed when we *don't* follow our natural instincts in situations that don't go our way.

## *Stewardship of Time*

Love one another. Submit to one another. Bear with one another. Prefer one another. Biblical commands such as these can cause us to think Christians are called to go through life as people pleasers. Then we read Galatians 1:10: "Am I now seeking the favor of people, or of God? Or am I striving to please people? If I were still trying to please people, I would not be a bond-servant of Christ."

Which is it? Trying to please others over ourselves or seeking God's approval? Is our behavior motivated by the desire for the approval of others or of God?

If I desire to please the Lord before anyone else, then yes, I am indeed called to place others' interests ahead of my own. Not because I seek their approval but because God calls me to do it. He is my "audience of one"—the one whose opinion matters above all others.

The trap of people pleasing is often revealed in how we use our time. I step into this trap whenever I say yes to the requests of others, wanting to please them, without first asking God what He wants me to do. As a result, sharing the fruit of self-control in how we spend our time may be misunderstood by others who want us to follow their agendas.

## *The Power of Words*

For many years I possessed an amazing skill: my ability to respond to negative comments with biting words. I justified my responses as defending myself with the truth.

Then the Holy Spirit began working in this area of my life. As I surrendered—and continue to surrender—my biting words have been replaced with biting my tongue! Cultivating self-control continues to teach me that not everything I'm thinking needs to be said, true or not. Words have the power to inflict pain. Once spoken, they don't vanish just because we've had a change of heart. I learned the hard way that a word carelessly spoken in a moment can have ramifications in the form of broken relationships for years to come.

If ever an area of our lives required self-control, it's the words we share with others. Yet James 3:8 tells us no one can tame their tongue. That sounds hopeless, doesn't it? If no one can tame their tongue, what's the solution?

We can't do it, but God can. The same God who parted the Red Sea, who brought down the walls of Jericho, and who raised Christ from the dead. When we yield to the Holy Spirit's control, our words can bring life instead of destruction. Proverbs 18:21 tells us, "Death and life are in the power of the tongue." We can speak words of praise and thanksgiving to God. We can speak the truth in love. And we can share the fruit of self-control by speaking words of kindness and encouragement, even when our own plans are frustrated.[13]

True self-control will always be the direct result of constant and continuous submission to the Holy Spirit. He is the only source of power sufficient to enable us to share this fruit through our authenticity, responses, time, and words.

## APPLICATION QUESTIONS

1. Which of the four temptations are you most susceptible to: selfishness, unbridled emotions, the blame game, or dismantling God's boundaries?
2. Were you surprised that self-control is a character quality of God? Why or why not?

3. Why is self-control foundational to our ability to live out *all* the fruit of the Spirit?
4. What is the status of your own "walls of self-control"? Where are the breaches?
5. How does self-control free you to reflect Christ?
6. Do you think of self-control as a gift? Why or why not?
7. What prevents you from fully applying the gift of this fruit in your life?
8. How do you reconcile the apostle Peter's urging to "make every effort" to develop self-control with the fact that self-control is a gift?
9. How easy or difficult is it for you to be authentic as opposed to stoic when you are hurting?
10. Are you more like Peter in his early days when he struggled with self-control or in his later days when he valued this fruit of the Spirit? How does submission to the Holy Spirit help you in this area?

# Epilogue

I love one-and-done tasks. The kind you take care of once and never have to revisit. However, reclaiming fruit targeted by the enemy is not a onetime activity. Satan constantly prowls, seeking to weaken our relationship with God and with others. We need to stay alert. As author Eva Marie Everson described in her book *The Third Path*, "Satan does not want for us to enjoy all God has to offer."[1]

The good news is that while the battles may continue, the war has already been won. Christ's victory on the cross is our victory too. The same power that raised Jesus from the dead is present in every follower of Christ by the indwelling Holy Spirit. Take heart! As Paul wrote in Romans 8:31–37:

> What then shall we say to these things? If God is for us, who is against us? He who did not spare His own Son, but delivered Him over for us all, how will He not also with Him freely give us all things? Who will bring charges against God's elect? God is the one who justifies; who is the one who condemns? Christ Jesus is He who died, but rather, was raised, who is at the right hand of God, who also intercedes for us. Who will separate us from the love of Christ? Will tribulation, or trouble, or persecution, or famine, or nakedness, or danger, or sword? . . . But in all these things we overwhelmingly conquer through Him who loved us.

Dwell on the lavishness of this thought for a moment. "We overwhelmingly conquer through Him who loved us." And speaking of love, you may have noticed that of the nine displays of the fruit of the Spirit, it's not by chance that love is listed first. The remaining displays of fruit—joy, peace, patience, kindness, goodness, faithfulness, gentleness, and self-control—are all ways we reveal our love to others. Paul made a similar observation in Colossians 3:12–14:

> As those who have been chosen of God, holy and beloved, put on a heart of compassion, kindness, humility, gentleness, and patience; bearing with one another, and forgiving each other, whoever has a complaint against anyone; just as the Lord forgave you, so must you do also. In addition to all these things put on love, which is the perfect bond of unity.

First John 4:8 and 4:19 explain that God is love, and because He first loved us, we love Him and those around us. So how do we manifest this love? Let's look again at the rich, descriptive phrases in 1 Corinthians 13:4–8 explaining the nature and characteristics of love. Notice how the adjectives Paul chose are associated with the fruit of the Spirit:

> Love is patient, love is kind, it is not jealous; love does not brag, it is not arrogant. It does not act disgracefully, it does not seek its own benefit; it is not provoked, does not keep an account of a wrong suffered, it does not rejoice in unrighteousness, but rejoices with the truth; it keeps every confidence, it believes all things, hopes all things, endures all things.
>
> Love never fails.

Patience, kindness, self-control ("not provoked"), goodness ("does not rejoice in unrighteousness"), joy ("rejoices with the truth"), and faithfulness ("endures all things"). All tied to love.

Every display of the fruit of the Spirit—love, joy, peace, patience, kindness, goodness, faithfulness, gentleness, and self-control—is an attribute God delights to develop in us by His Holy Spirit. Let's ask Him to show us which ones most need cultivating in our lives. Rather than trying harder to develop these characteristics ourselves, let's submit to the Holy Spirit and cooperate with the work He is doing in those areas. As He works in us, we can echo Paul's words in Ephesians 3:20–21:

> To Him who is able to do far more abundantly beyond all that we ask or think, according to the power that works within us, to Him be the glory in the church and in Christ Jesus to all generations forever and ever. Amen.

# Acknowledgments

Thank you to

. . . the prayer team who faithfully prayed for more than two years as I completed this labor of love.

. . . the members of Word Weavers International and other friends who provided candid, much-appreciated feedback.

. . . Bob Hostetler, who believed in this book, represented it, and suggested the title, *Flourish*.

. . . the Kregel Publications team, who saw the potential in *Flourish* to encourage God's people in claiming the fruit promised to us by the Holy Spirit.

. . . the Lord most of all, whose Holy Spirit gives us His fruit and seals us in love as a deposit guaranteeing our inheritance to the praise of His glory.

# Notes

## *Chapter 1: The Status Quo Has Got to Go!*

1. John 14:16–17.
2. Revelation 12:10; 1 Thessalonians 3:5; 1 Peter 5:8; Genesis 3:1.
3. J. I. Packer, *Keep in Step with the Spirit: Finding Fullness in Our Walk with God*, rev. ed. (Baker Books, 2005), 15.
4. Neil T. Anderson and Robert L. Saucy, *The Common Made Holy: Being Conformed to the Image of God* (Harvest House, 1997), 283.
5. Jerry Bridges, *The Pursuit of Holiness* (NavPress, 1978), 83.
6. Edie Melson, "The Transforming Breath of God," *Arise Daily Devotions*, May 19, 2024, https://arisedailydevos.wordpress.com/2024/05/19/the-transforming-breath-of-god-/.
7. John 12:31; 16:11.
8. 1 Peter 5:9; James 4:7.
9. 2 Corinthians 2:11.
10. 1 John 3:8.
11. 1 John 2:16.
12. Ephesians 5:18.
13. Ephesians 4:3; 5:18.
14. John 14:6.
15. Ephesians 6:17.
16. Warren Wiersbe, *Matthew–Galatians*, Bible Exposition Commentary New Testament, vol. 1 (Cook Communications, 2001), 720.

## *Chapter 2: The Heart of Our Fruit Is Love*

1. C. S. Lewis, *The Screwtape Letters* (New American Library, 1988), 47.
2. Romans 12:3.
3. Romans 8:29.
4. Matthew 5:44.
5. Bill Crowder, *Before Christmas: The Story of Jesus from the Beginning of Time to the Manger* (Discovery House, 2019), 50.
6. Ephesians 1:3–8.
7. Romans 8:5.
8. Romans 12:2.
9. 2 Corinthians 10:5.
10. Philippians 4:8.
11. Matthew 22:37.
12. John Musyimi, "5 Ways to Love God with All Your Mind," The Gospel Coalition Africa, January 7, 2020, https://africa.thegospelcoalition.org/article/love-god-with-all-your-mind/.
13. Julie Ackerman Link, *Loving God with All My Heart* (Discovery House, 2004), 26.
14. Ephesians 1:4–5.
15. John 14:23.
16. J. I. Packer, *Keep in Step with the Spirit: Finding Fullness in Our Walk with God*, rev. ed. (Baker Books, 2005), 114.
17. Jon Bloom, "If We Love God Most, We Will Love Others Best," Desiring God, June 24, 2016, www.desiringgod.org/articles/if-we-love-god-most-we-will-love-others-best.
18. James 1:22.
19. Oswald Chambers, *My Utmost for His Highest: An Updated Edition in Today's Language*, ed. James Reimann (Discovery House, 1992), May 11.
20. Matthew 22:39.
21. Joseph Stowell, *The Final Question of Jesus: How You Can Live the Answer Today* (Multnomah, 2004), 64.

22. Elisabeth Elliot, *The Mark of a Man: Following Christ's Example of Masculinity* (Revell, 1981), 104.
23. 1 John 4:11.

## Chapter 3: The Song of Our Fruit Is Joy

1. 2 Corinthians 4:4.
2. Nehemiah 8:10.
3. Exodus 20:13, 17.
4. "They've cracked it at last! The chicken DID come before the egg," Daily Mail, July 14, 2010, https://www.dailymail.co.uk/sciencetech/article-1294341/Chicken-really-DID-come-egg-say-scientists.html.
5. Ephesians 2:10.
6. Romans 5:15–17.
7. 1 Thessalonians 4:13.
8. 2 Corinthians 5:17–20.
9. 2 Corinthians 7:4.
10. Charles Haddon Spurgeon, "Joy, a Duty," sermon, Metropolitan Tabernacle, London, March 20, 1887, https://www.spurgeon.org/resource-library/sermons/joy-a-duty/#flipbook/.
11. Philippians 2:2.

## Chapter 4: The Soul of Our Fruit Is Peace

1. Steve Carter, *The Thing Beneath the Thing: What's Hidden Inside (and What God Helps Us Do About It)* (Thomas Nelson, 2021), 139.
2. Isaiah 14:12–14.
3. Jim Elliot, quoted in Elisabeth Elliot, *Shadow of the Almighty: The Life and Testament of Jim Elliot* (Hendrickson, 2008), 112.
4. See Luke 12:2–3.
5. Adapted from Berit Kjos, *A Wardrobe from the King: 8 Studies on the Armor of God* (Victor Books, 1988), 45–46.
6. A. W. Tozer, *The Knowledge of the Holy* (HarperCollins, 1961), 1.

7. Isaiah 9:6.
8. Britt Mooney, *We Were Reborn for This: The Jesus Model for Living Heaven on Earth* (Bold Vision Books, 2023), 118.
9. 1 Peter 5:7.
10. Romans 5:10.
11. Ava Pennington, *Reflections on the Names of God: 180 Devotions to Know God More Fully* (Revell, 2010), 54.
12. 2 Corinthians 5:18.
13. Tozer, *Knowledge of the Holy*, 1.

### *Chapter 5: The Test of Our Fruit Is Patience*

1. John 4:34; 17:11, 24; Matthew 28:19.
2. Genesis 1:27; 2 Corinthians 3:18.
3. 1 Samuel 10:8.
4. Jonah 4:1–2.
5. Matthew 18:21–35.
6. Genesis 15:6.
7. Genesis 12:4; 16:3.
8. Genesis 16:2.
9. J. D. Watson, *A Word for the Day: Key Words from the New Testament* (AMG Publishers, 2006), 284.
10. John Donne, "Meditation XVII," in *Devotions upon Emergent Occasions* [. . .], 1624, public domain.
11. 1 Timothy 1:16; Romans 2:4; 2 Peter 3:9, 15.
12. Genesis 5:32 tells us Noah was five hundred years old when he became the father of three sons. In 6:18, God told Noah that he and his family, including his sons and their wives, would enter the ark. And 7:6 tells us Noah was six hundred years old when the floodwaters came.
13. Genesis 37, 39.
14. Cindy K. Sproles, email message to author, January 22, 2024. Used by permission.
15. John 13:5–17.

## Chapter 6: The Generosity of Our Fruit Is Kindness

1. James Strong, *The New Strong's Complete Dictionary of Bible Words* (Thomas Nelson, 1996), under "*chrēstotēs.*"
2. Strong, *New Strong's Complete Dictionary*, under "*chrēstos.*"
3. Jeremiah 25:12.
4. John Walvoord and Roy Zuck, eds., *The Bible Knowledge Commentary: New Testament* (Cook Communications, 2000), 681.
5. Philippians 4:6–8.
6. Ava Pennington, *One Year Alone with God: 366 Devotions on the Names of God* (Revell, 2010), 358.
7. Ephesians 4:32.
8. Job 2:11–13.

## Chapter 7: The Virtue of Our Fruit Is Goodness

1. Ephesians 2:2.
2. James 1:17.
3. Genesis 3.
4. John 10:11.
5. *Letters of C. S. Lewis*, ed. W. H. Lewis (Harcourt, 1966), 477.
6. Aimee Nelson, message given at LifeQuest Church Ladies' Breakfast, Palm City, FL, May 6, 2023. Used by permission.
7. C. S. Lewis, *Mere Christianity* (HarperCollins, 2001), 63.
8. Matthew 23:13.
9. Ephesians 2:8–9.
10. Quoted in Ava Pennington, *Daily Reflections on the Names of God: A Devotional* (Revell, 2013), 360.
11. J. I. Packer, *Knowing God* (InterVarsity Press, 1973), 165.
12. Ecclesiastes 12:13.
13. 1 Corinthians 10:24.
14. Romans 8:29.
15. Luke 6:32–35.

## Chapter 8: The Devotion of Our Fruit Is Faithfulness

1. Oswald Chambers, *My Utmost for His Highest: An Updated*

*Edition in Today's Language*, ed. James Reimann (Discovery House, 1992), October 11.

2. A. W. Tozer, *The Knowledge of the Holy* (HarperCollins, 1961), 81.
3. Malachi 3:6; Hebrews 13:8.
4. Brad Bigney, *Gospel Treason: Betraying the Gospel with Hidden Idols* (P&R Publishing, 2012), 24.
5. Exodus 14:21–22.
6. Exodus 15:22–24; 16:1–3.
7. Jim Elliot, in a journal entry from October 28, 1949, quoted in Justin Taylor, "They Were No Fools: The Martrydom of Jim Elliot and Four Other Missionaries," The Gospel Coalition, January 8, 2016, https://www.thegospelcoalition.org/blogs/justin-taylor/they-were-no-fools-60-years-ago-today-the-martyrdom-of-jim-elliot-and-four-other-missionaries/.
8. Thomas Chisolm, "Great Is Thy Faithfulness," 1923, public domain.
9. 1 Corinthians 4:2.
10. Randy Alcorn, *The Treasure Principle: Unlocking the Secret of Joyful Giving* (Multnomah, 2008), 25.
11. Job 41:11; Psalm 24:1.
12. Elisabeth Elliot, *Discipline: The Glad Surrender* (Revell, 1982), 97.
13. Elliot, *Discipline*, 99.

## *Chapter 9: The Character of Our Fruit Is Gentleness*

1. Compare with Isaiah 42:1–4.
2. *The Princess Bride*, written by William Goldman, directed by Rob Reiner, featuring Cary Elwes, Mandy Patinkin, and Robin Wright, 1987, Twentieth Century Fox.
3. *The Hebrew-Greek Key Word Study Bible: Bringing the Original Text to Life*, ed. Spiros Zodhiates and Warren Baker (AMG Publishers, 2008), under "*praütēs*."
4. Steve Brown, *The Spirit of Freedom* (Key Life Network, n.d.), 20.
5. Cleon L. Rogers Jr. and Cleon L. Rogers III, eds., *The New*

*Linguistic and Exegetical Key to the Greek New Testament* (Zondervan, 1998), 9.

6. Galatians 6:1.
7. Elisabeth Elliot, *A Lamp unto My Feet: The Bible's Light for Your Daily Walk* (Revell, 2004), 44.
8. 2 Timothy 2:25.

## *Chapter 10: The Discipline of Our Fruit Is Self-Control*

1. *Strong's*, "G1828—*exelkō*," Blue Letter Bible, https://www.blueletterbible.org/lexicon/g1828/niv/mgnt/0-1/.
2. *Strong's*, "G1185—*deleazō*," Blue Letter Bible, https://www.blueletterbible.org/lexicon/g1185/niv/mgnt/0-1/.
3. Warren Wiersbe, *Matthew–Galatians*, Bible Exposition Commentary New Testament, vol. 1 (Cook Communications, 2001), 501.
4. Herbert Lockyer Sr., ed., *Illustrated Dictionary of the Bible* (Thomas Nelson, 1986), 1091.
5. *The Archaeological Study Bible* (Zondervan, 2005), 1001.
6. Elisabeth Elliot, *Discipline: The Glad Surrender* (Revell, 1982), 18.
7. Elliot, *Discipline*, 28.
8. J. D. Watson, *A Word for the Day: Key Words from the New Testament* (AMG Publishers, 2006), 253.
9. John Walvoord and Roy Zuck, eds., *The Bible Knowledge Commentary: New Testament* (Cook, 2000), 865.
10. John 17:17, 20.
11. Elliot, *Discipline*, 151.
12. Britt Mooney, *We Were Reborn for This: The Jesus Model for Living Heaven on Earth* (Bold Vision Books, 2023), 172–73.
13. Adapted from "Power of the Tongue," *Ava Pennington* (blog), June 1, 2023, www.avapennington.com/2023/the-power-of-the-tongue/.

## *Epilogue*

1. Eva Marie Everson, *The Third Path: Finding Intimacy with God on the Path of Questioning* (Bold Vision Books, 2022), 82.

# About the Author

Ava Pennington is an author, speaker, Bible teacher, and teaching leader for Bible Study Fellowship International. She has a master's from St. John's University and a certification in Adult Bible Studies from Moody Bible Institute. A member of the Christian Author's Network (CAN) and the Advanced Writers and Speakers Association (AWSA), she has authored *Reflections on the Names of God* and the complementary *Daily Reflections on the Names of God*. She loves connecting with audiences through relevant, challenging, and enjoyable presentations. Find out more at avapennington.com.